START BEING FEARLESS, STOP BEING SCARED

RACHEL STONE

Copyright © 2021 by Rachel Stone

All rights reserved.

No part of this book may be reproduced in any form or by any electronic or mechanical means, including information storage and retrieval systems, without written permission from the author, except for the use of brief quotations in a book review.

Claim Your Freebie NOW!

Get Good At Problem Solving

Want to know the secret behind getting good at problem solving? Everyone seems to be able to do it, but you're stuck in the pile of endless to-do lists with little progress.

Ok, so how do I get my FREE book?

EASY! See the next page

Claim Your Freebie NOW

Instructions:

1. Open the camera or the QR reader application on your smartphone.
2. Point your camera at the QR code to scan the QR code.
3. A notification will pop-up on screen.
4. Click on the notification to open the website link

Also By Rachel Stone

How To Remove Negativity From Your Life

Rid yourself forever from the negative thoughts that plague your life with this amazing, life-changing book.

Also By Rachel Stone

Why Living a Simple Life is Better for You

An easy guide to help you change the way you think about your life. Take steps to start living a stress-free life.

Also By Rachel Stone

How To Heal Toxic Thoughts

Are you sick of your whole day being ruined due to your overthinking? Have you had enough of self-sabotaging everything good in your life? Do you want practical strategies to finally have a peaceful night's sleep?

Grab the Rachel Stone series NOW

Instructions:

1. Open the camera or the QR reader application on your smartphone.
2. Point your camera at the QR code to scan the QR code.
3. A notification will pop-up on screen.
4. Click on the notification to open the website link

Grobby Reebok Shops Sore NOW

Hurry, hurry,

1. Download a copy of the QR reader application on your smartphone
2. Ensure you are on campus or in the UK come to see the zhoode LA Boulevards wi pn sqr np 260
3. Open it (the app) then to open the camera, or

SCAN ME

Contents

Introduction	xix
1. THE FEAR CHARACTERISTICS	**1**
What Exactly Is Fear?	1
Myths Around Fear	3
What Exactly Does The Term "Fearless" Imply?	5
2. IT'S TIME TO FACE YOUR DEEPEST FEARS	**8**
The Modern World's Survival	9
What Are We Afraid Of?	10
The Distinction Between Fearlessness And Bravery	11
3. FEAR OF REJECTION	**13**
The Outcast's Prototype	14
Positive Characteristics	16
Behaviours And Habits	16
The Voice Of The Outcast	17
How This Fear Can Hold You Back	18
Methods For Overcoming This Fear	19
Getting Over Rejection	20
4. FEAR OF MAKING A MISTAKE	**22**
The Procrastinator's Prototype	23
Positive Characteristics	24
Behaviours And Habits	25
The Voice Of The Procrastinator	25
How This Fear Can Hold You Back	26
Methods For Overcoming This Fear	27
Going Above And Beyond Perfection	28
5. FEAR OF COLOURING OUTSIDE THE LINES	**30**
The Rule Follower's Prototype	32
Positive Characteristics	33
Behaviours And Habits	33
The Voice Of The Rule Follower	34
How This Fear Can Hold You Back	34

Methods For Overcoming This Fear	35
Getting Over The Fear Of Breaking The Rules	37

6. FEAR OF WHAT OTHER PEOPLE WILL THINK — 39
The People Pleaser Prototype	40
Positive Characteristics	41
Behaviours And Habits	42
The Voice Of The People Pleaser	42
How This Fear Can Hold You Back	43
Methods for Overcoming This Fear	44
Getting Over The Need To Please	46

7. FEAR OF NOT BEING GOOD ENOUGH — 47
The Self-Doubter Prototype	49
Positive Characteristics	50
Behaviours And Habits	50
The Voice Of The Self-Doubter	51
How This Fear Can Hold You Back?	52
Methods For Overcoming This Fear	53
Getting Over Insecurity	54

8. FEAR OF TAKING RESPONSIBILITY — 56
The Excuse Maker's Prototype	58
Positive Characteristics	59
Behaviours And Habits	59
The Voice Of The Excuse Maker	60
How This Fear Can Hold You Back	61
Methods For Overcoming This Fear	62
Getting Rid Of Excuses	63

9. FEAR OF ADVERSITY — 65
The Pessimist Prototype	67
Positive Characteristics	68
Behaviours And Habits	68
How This Fear Can Hold You Back	70
Methods For Overcoming This Fear	71
Getting Over Pessimism	73

10. CONTINUE TO BE OPTIMISTIC — 74
Beware Of The Space Between	75
Modify The Script	76
Continue Filling Up	77

Practice Self-Care	78
Every Victory Should Be Celebrated	79
Feedback	81
Claim Your Freebie NOW!	83
Claim Your Freebie NOW	85
Also By Rachel Stone	87
Also By Rachel Stone	89
Also By Rachel Stone	91
Grab the Rachel Stone series NOW	93

Introduction

Most of us live a life that is filled with both beautiful and painful experiences. But, for many of us, even when we are at our happiest, there is dread lurking under the surface. We are afraid that this time will pass us by, that we will not obtain what we need, that we will lose what we cherish, or that we will not be safe. Our greatest fear is often the awareness that one day our bodies will stop working. So, even when we have all of the conditions for happiness, our joy is incomplete.

We believe that to be joyful; we should push our fears aside or ignore them. We don't feel at ease when we think about the things that make us nervous, so we ignore our fear. "Oh, no, I'm not going to worry about that." We attempt to ignore our dread, yet it persists.

The only way to alleviate our fear and be joyful is to accept it and investigate its origins thoroughly. Instead of attempting to flee our fear, we may bring it to our awareness and examine it honestly and thoroughly. We are terrified of things outside of ourselves over which we have no control. We are concerned about becoming ill, ageing, and losing the things we value the most. We strive to hang on to what is important to us—our jobs, property, and loved ones. But clenching our fists does little to alleviate our anxiety. We will eventually have to let go of all of them. We won't be able to take them with us.

Concurrently, the thinking process creates a subconscious perimeter that imprisons the part of us that wants to succeed by mistaking the sense of adrenalin for fear. Fear is what keeps people in their ordinary lives. Fear is believed to be dispelled by knowledge. Take a careful look at yourself, as well as at yourself. How many individuals do you know who are content with their position in life?

Society is full of underachievers: not because we lack talent or bravery, but because we don't understand our own physical reactions to confrontation. Adrenaline frequently causes panic, forcing plans to be abandoned or modified out of dread of the repercussions or fear of the fear itself.

'If you know your enemy and know yourself, you need not fear the outcome of a hundred battles,' said General Sun Tzu 25 centuries ago. Knowing oneself entails realising that fear is both a friend and an adversary. It's okay to be scared; we're all scared. And we require it to ensure the survival of our species. Fear is a friend in this way; it can be managed and used as a life-changing fuel. Only when we panic does fear become a mind-killer.

'Life is not a rehearsal,' said Ian Botham. We only have one chance to achieve something amazing, important, and life-changing — and this is it. The majority of individuals are living lives they do not wish to live. Why? Because they are trapped in safe bet comfort zones that they are afraid to leave for fear of failure, success, change, danger, ridicule, or anything. They fantasise about better professions, happier relationships, fancier vehicles, prosperity, and fulfilment, but such goals are rarely achieved because FEAR lurks in the shadows between dream and reality. The excuse syndrome is commonly used to shift blame for failure. 'If it wasn't for..., I could do a lot more with my life.' Most of us wait in the driveway of life, too terrified to pull out into traffic, too hesitant to burn gas, and too fearful of crashing. Many people have the dynamite to live an exciting life but lack the courage and insight to light the fuse.

Most people fail to realise that whether you are confronting a major commercial transaction, a discussion with your boss, or a pair of muggers across an alleyway, you will experience fear. It is as much the unexpectedness of the sensation as it is the experience itself that converts men to mice. When faced with a confrontation of any type, we will experience fear, and its manifestation will take numerous forms with varying degrees of severity. It'll always be there.

This book aims to educate people on the mechanics of fear to assist break down prison walls. How to recognise, comprehend, and then control fear to be used as an ally. This is not a book on phobias; however, the symptoms and treatments are similar to those of the phobic condition. Exposure treatment has the same results when coping with fear at all levels. One addresses fear methodically until desensitisation develops.

1

The Fear Characteristics

WHEN IT COMES to confronting the barriers that hold us back or prevent us from achieving our goals and ambitions, not all fear is created equal, nor does it always appear in the same manner. The seven fear prototypes illustrate the various ways fear may manifest itself in our lives.

The good news is that once we recognise the sort of fear that is negatively affecting our lives, holding us back, or keeping us trapped, we can act.

What Exactly Is Fear?

What exactly is fear? What can be said about it? According to the English dictionary, fear is "an unpleasant, frequently intense feeling produced by anticipation or consciousness of danger." When the brain detects danger, it releases adrenalin, a human turbo charge caused by awareness and anticipation to help in fight or flight. This powerful unpleasant feeling frequently induces panic immobilisation in the recipient, also known as the freeze syndrome. Adrenaline functions similarly to fuel injection or turbo drive in a sports vehicle, with action serving as the metaphorical accelerator. You activate the turbo and accelerate the vehicle by pressing the accelerator and engaging the clutch in an automobile.

However, if you sit at a traffic light and push your foot on the accelerator without engaging the clutch, there will be no movement, and you will waste fuel. Similarly, when we engage in action (fight or flight) in reaction to fear, we activate adrenalin's turbo drive, triggering a quick and spontaneous response. However, if we do not take action and panic sets in, the extra energy will overwhelm us.

When you are willing to meet fear face to face, you open yourself up to the chance to feel the fear and allow it to unfold in front of you, revealing that the fear is nothing when completely confronted! The greatest fear was of the fear of itself. The intriguing aspect is that, even if you dismiss your concerns, they are just pushed to the side and only appear at the most inconvenient (or reasonable) times. You could find yourself shoving this fear away as soon as possible.

Assume you have a fear of public speaking and are offered the chance to speak to an audience of 300 people about a subject that you are completely passionate about through your business or employment. For some of you reading this, the anxiety may be so overpowering from the moment of the offer that you say "No thanks" to this incredible chance.

Others may discover you saying "Yes" and wondering how you would cope with it afterwards.

Tomorrow comes to the speaking event, and you toss and turn in bed that night, your stomach churning, wondering whether you have food poisoning or a stomach upset (you may even find yourself hoping this is true!). Fear has emerged to be addressed at this time! So, rather than pushing through the fear, STOP, even if just for 12 seconds, and be still, willing to confront it.

If you find it difficult to stop at first, you might ask yourself, "What am I most afraid of right now?" You could be shocked at what ideas arise; it could be of embarrassment, that others will not appreciate what you have to say, or something completely different. I frequently push the fear to its limit by asking myself, "What if nobody ever approved of me again?" The fear then leaps forward to be confronted. So, at this time of confronting fear, STOP! STOP

RIGHT NOW! When patterns of wanting to move on fast or change the subject emerge, you may deliberately choose to let them pass as you STOP and watch them. There is no need to change anything; simply notice how the energy flows throughout the body and then abruptly decreases, allowing you to experience a feeling commonly characterised as expansiveness, emptiness, quiet, serenity, and love.

This is not intended to be a new notion or strategy for the mind but rather a chance to connect with fear and pass naturally. Whatever your fear is, be willing to STOP and feel it in the present now. When we dismiss any emotion, even fear, the energy and lesson are stored inside the body and frequently manifest later. So why not take advantage of the chance to meet it as it presents itself?

When you allow emotions to be present, you may discover that tales begin to emerge as well! You may even notice that a slew of new tales begins to emerge. The narrative of blame ("he/she did this to me"), guilt ("it's all because I did that horrible thing"), and justified anger ("I have a reason to be upset about this"). Simply notice the stories as they occur; when you are ready to clean or complete patterns in your life, the mind may reveal numerous memories. So, as best you can, watch the stories and allow them to run through you, and notice that when you don't dive into the stories, they fade away, as do the feelings.

Myths Around Fear

What is your relationship with fear? What I mean is, how has your perception of terror influenced your life and choices? If you've ever considered taking a major risk or making a change to improve your life or work, you've probably experienced feelings of fear and anxiety. When we move outside of our comfort zone and face our fears, we have a very particular reaction known as the fight or flight response. Whether you were millions of years ago and a woolly mammoth charged at you, you had two choices: run or hold your ground and fight. Both take a significant amount of energy. Consider this: our fight or flight reflex comes in at the first sign of a threat—a quick movement in the bushes.

When we desire to create a positive change, we experience the same fight or flight response. The problem is that most people are unaware of what is going on, and they give fear and worry much too much influence over their lives.

Here are four fear myths that will transform your life:

MYTH 1: Fear is a sign of weakness

When we are afraid, it is natural for us to feel that way. If you don't react when you take a risk, confront a challenge, or leave your comfort zone, something is wrong.

MYTH 2: Fear reduces performance.

Any great athlete, movie star, or public speaker will tell you that they have a fight or flight reaction. Top achievers, on the other hand, rarely employ terms like fear or worry. They've learned a vital truth: Fear is not your adversary. It is a potent source of energy that may be harnessed and utilised to your advantage.

MYTH 3: Fear is what keeps you back.

The story goes that fear prevents you from accomplishing your goals in life. In reality, this is not the case. What is holding you back is not fear but rather your attitude toward fear. The more you cling to the belief that fear is negative, the more you will be stuck and the more anxious you will get.

MYTH 4: Confidence is defined as the absence of fear.

According to popular belief, confident people are not anxious or afraid. The fact is that even the most self-assured people in the world experience fear in difficult circumstances. Genuine confidence is an altered relationship with fear, not the absence of fear.

What Exactly Does The Term "Fearless" Imply?

It entails understanding of how to use fear to your advantage. And to do so, you must first understand what you are dealing with.

1. Fear is a healthy emotion.

For a good reason, fear is built into your brain: neuroscientists have found separate networks that go from the limbic system to the prefrontal cortex and back. Even in the absence of a scary trigger, they induce fear when these networks are electrically or chemically activated. Fear is neither aberrant nor a sign of weakness: the ability to be scared is a natural element of brain function. A lack of fear may indicate severe brain injury.

2. There are several hues of fear.

Fear is an unpleasant feeling that can range from moderate to paralysing, from anticipating the results of a medical exam to learning of a deadly terrorist assault. Terrifying situations might leave a lifelong impact on your brain circuitry, necessitating professional assistance. Chronic stress, a low-intensity kind of fear manifested as free-floating anxiety, persistent concern, and everyday uncertainty, can, on the other hand, silently but significantly impair your physical and mental health over time.

3. Fear is not as automatic as you may believe.

Fear is partly instinctive, partly acquired, and partly taught. Some fears are instinctive: Because of the consequences for survival, pain, for example, induces fear. Other fears are discovered: Because of bad connections and prior experiences, we learn to be scared of particular individuals, locations, or circumstances. A near-drowning event, for example, may make you uncomfortable whenever you get close to a body of water. Other fears are instilled in students: Cultural norms frequently influence whether or not something should be feared. Consider how some social groupings are feared and punished due to a societally constructed perception that they are harmful.

4. You don't have to be in danger to feel terrified.

Fear is also partially imagined; thus, it can emerge in the absence of something scary. Indeed, since our brains are so efficient, we come to fear various stimuli that are not terrifying (conditioned fear) or are not even there (anticipatory anxiety). We are afraid because of what we think could happen. According to some neuroscientists, humans are the most scared species on the planet due to our ability to learn, think, and generate fear in our brains. However, this low-grade, objectless fear can develop into persistent anxiety over nothing in particular, becoming debilitating.

5. The more terrified you are, the scarier things will appear.

If you are already in a state of fear, your fear reaction is enhanced through a process known as potentiation. When you are predisposed to fear, even innocuous situations might appear frightening. A tickling on your neck produced by a loose thread in your sweater can shock you and lead you to jump out of your seat in a panic if you watch a documentary about deadly spiders. Even the tiniest turbulence can send your blood pressure through the roof of the plane if you are scared of flying. And the more concerned you are about your job security, the more nervous you will be when your employer invites you for even a routine meeting.

6. Your behaviours are dictated by your fear.

Fear-motivated actions are classified into four categories: **freeze**, **fight**, **flight**, and **fright**. When you **freeze**, you stop what you're doing and focus on the frightening stimuli to decide what to do next (e.g., you read a memo that your company will be laying off people). Then you must decide whether to use **fight** or **flight**. It would help if you decided whether to confront the threat head-on (explain to your employer why you should not be laid off) or to work around it (start looking for another job). When the fear becomes overpowering, you experience **fright**: you do not fight or flee; in fact, you do nothing—well, you worry about the issue, ruminate, and moan, but you do not act. Constantly being in fright mode might lead to pessimism and depression.

7. The more serious the threat, the bolder your acts are.

We have varied reactions to real and imagined threats. Imagined dangers cause paralysis. Fear of all the horrible things that could or might not happen in the future causes you to worry a lot but take little action. You're trapped in a state of panic, overwhelmed but unsure what to do. True threats, on the other hand, create a frenzy. When a threat is imminent and identifiable, you respond quickly and without hesitation. This is why people are considerably more likely to modify their eating habits after a major health threat (e.g., a heart attack) than after just reading data about the negative effects of a fried-food diet. You must put yourself at risk if you want to motivate your troops.

FEAR MAY BE both a friend and an adversary. And the fear of fear may keep you imprisoned in an insecure cage. How do you get over it? You learn how to use it.

2

It's Time To Face Your Deepest Fears

ONE OF THE most potent factors in your life is **fear**. It impacts the decisions you make, the activities you do, and the results you obtain. Fear has affected who you are and what you do at some time in your life. Being successful is heavily reliant on learning how to use fear to your advantage.

Fear is necessary for survival. It is a hardwired, basic emotion that includes multiple brain regions (not just the amygdala) and results in a complicated experience characterised by a specific pattern of mental and physiological activity.

Fear is an internal – mainly automatic (but not totally) – alarm system designed to warn against risks to one's existence. In the past, survival meant just remaining alive. It meant avoiding death at the hands of a predator, an illness, a rival, or a natural calamity. Threats comprised everything that may genuinely result in death or serious injury. Our forefathers were kept safe by their fear.

However, as the world's complexity and demand rose, the meaning of both survival and threat shifted considerably. What does survival entail nowadays, and what is the greatest threat to it?

The Modern World's Survival

All fears, no matter how great or little, fall into five categories, according to author Karl Albrecht:

1. Fear of extinction
2. Fear of mutilation
3. Fear of losing autonomy
4. Fear of separation
5. Fear of ego-death

As a result, fear's purpose in these five areas is to promote survival. To defend ourselves against anything that threatens our lives and our bodily and psychological well-being, autonomy, and connection to others. So, in the context of our complicated social, cultural, political, and technical environment, the following apply:

BIOLOGICAL SURVIVAL: The urge to survive is still the priority. Everything else is meaningless unless you are living. When your life is in danger, the fear alarm sounds the loudest.

PHYSICAL HEALTH AND ABILITY: Being healthy and strong is important for biological existence and for meeting the demands of daily living. This is why millions of people receive flu jabs each year and why hand sanitiser is in every handbag.

AUTONOMY: We desire the freedom to make our own decisions and live as we see fit. We don't enjoy being held back, either literally or metaphorically. This is what makes being stuck, whether in an elevator or a bad job, so terrifying and why the fear of jail serves as a strong deterrent to breaking the law.

We desire to belong and stay linked to surviving socially. Acceptance and respect from our peers. We attempt to avoid criticism and rejection from those we like or even strangers. It might be terrifying to be alone and to feel unloved and irrelevant. This is one of the reasons why people remain in abusive relationships or join gangs.

SELF-WORTH: Given how little time we have with ourselves, we must safeguard our self-worth at all costs. In every situation, low self-esteem is a major issue. Fear of feeling useless and incompetent may be crippling, preventing you from thinking big, expressing yourself, and taking risks. As a result, the effects of losing a job or receiving a rejection letter might linger for days or even weeks.

What Are We Afraid Of?

We have removed many of the dangers that threatened our forefathers' existence. However, fear persists. What makes people fearful in these times? Chapman University researchers polled 1,500 people to find out what they are most scared of. The top five fears were:

- Government corruption
- Cyber-terrorism
- Government and corporate surveillance of personal information
- Terrorist assaults
- Bio-warfare

These are indeed terrifying occurrences with severe and long-term repercussions. But are they the worries that keep you awake at night? Are these the fears that are preventing you from attaining your objectives? Is it your top goal to avoid government corruption or bioterrorism? What about losing your job, not having enough money to provide for your family, becoming ill without access to healthcare, being bullied at school or harassed at work, or failing to live by your values? These concerns may not be as explosive as terrorist attacks, but they can surely make your life miserable daily.

Survival requirements and the threats to them have evolved over millennia. Nonetheless, fear's role stays unchanged. To guard and warn. Fear may be unpleasant, even paralysing, at times. There are approximately 100 recognised phobias in the psychiatric literature, a disease defined by persistent and illogical fear of things or situations. You've probably heard of agoraphobia, claustrophobia, and social phobia. The good news is that fear is not pathological in the vast majority of individuals. It can, however, be as debilitating.

The fact is that you cannot and should not strive to eradicate fear. You may, however, remain fearless.

The Distinction Between Fearlessness And Bravery

In the lack of bravery and action, fear might be the most significant impediment to our achievement. On the other hand, fear may be a wonderful accelerator toward achievement if we face our fears and respond with bravery. When we think of the term "bravery," we see first responders rescuing people in times of tragedy, a mountain climber overcoming nature's difficulties while conquering Mount Everest, or a professional player pulling off a clutch win at the end of a crucial game. Bravery is the quality that drives people to tackle risky or difficult situations despite their fear. Courageous people take action despite their fears. Courage is more than merely climbing a mountain; no one has ever tried to climb or participate in risky sports and risk life and limb to become a hero. Brave individuals are not fearless; they experience fear but let it go by not concentrating on it.

Bravery does not imply the absence of fear. In reality, bravery necessitates fear. If you are not frightened of anything, there is no need to be brave. We will be afraid of a variety of things throughout our professions and lives. We would not be human if we did not experience fear. When you look at successful people who face their fears regularly, you will notice that they exude confidence. Courage comes to those who act, not those who wait, contemplate, or wonder! Courage, like other skill sets, may be cultivated, but it cannot be learned by attending a conference or reading a book.

The only way to acquire bravery is to do what you are afraid of. When you do things that terrify you, you grow, and those things scare you less and less until you wonder why they ever terrified you in the first place! We have all suffered from fear at some time in our lives. One trait I've noticed in the most prominent territory managers throughout my career is their capacity to show bravery in the face of fear. During training sessions, these individuals are the first to offer a role-play in front of their peers. These executives always take action to drive their company forward, never hesitating to approach a surgeon, ask for a reference, and seek the order. It's not that these salespeople aren't afraid of anything. It takes bravery to be scared and still act.

When you sit down to have lunch, you don't need bravery since there is no fear. When fear appears, we have the chance to call and experience bravery inside ourselves. I'll say it again: brave salesmen are not fearless; they sense fear and just let it go by not focusing on it. They focus their attention on more essential matters, such as their objectives.

True courage needs continuous practice. To go forward toward our goals, we must dig deep within ourselves and forget all we have been taught, everything we know, and everything we fear. Fear is a wake-up call. True bravery requires us to step beyond our comfort zones—it is about extending ourselves and not allowing our emotions to stand in the way of achieving greatness and fulfilment.

3

Fear Of Rejection

VICKY IS NOT the kind of person who would be described as "fearful."

She looks to be the polar opposite most of the time—completely fearless, a person who makes her own rules and lives life on her own terms. She is loud, self-assured, and daring. She marches to the beat of her own drum and appears to be unconcerned about what others say. She's always up for an adventure, likes to travel, and can't seem to stay in place.

She works as an independent contractor in the IT business, which provides her with a lot of freedom and independence and allows her to move around for short-term assignments. That's exactly how she likes it, since every time Vicky has attempted to work for someone else for more than a year or two, things haven't gone so well. Her ability to go in there and get the job done, even if it means ruffling a few feathers along the way, has always pleased the firms she has worked for. Vicky is never hesitant to speak up or say the controversial things that others are scared to utter aloud, yet her direct communication approach might lead her into problems at times.

The fact is that Vicky is distrustful of most people, and if asked, she will acknowledge she has trust issues. And, while she may be a lot of fun, she only has a few individuals in her life who she considers to be part of her inner circle—those she trusts enough to call genuine friends. Even yet, she is constantly upset when she feels left out or excluded—when her coworkers go out for drinks after work or make weekend plans, and she is not invited. She acts as if she doesn't care, but she does.

Vicky was raised amid three sisters, and she always felt like the family's black sheep. Her two sisters were both athletic and popular, and they have liked them, even her parents, while Vicky always felt that she didn't fit in. She was more interested in the "geeky" stuff, as her sisters referred to it—drama club, computers, and art—activities that the rest of her family didn't seem to understand or enjoy.

And, while she was aware that her family cared for her, she never felt completely loved or accepted by them. They looked too preoccupied with attending every soccer, volleyball, and basketball event to bother with art exhibits or robotics competitions. Vicky attempted to seem as if she didn't care, but deep down, she did.

She began to embrace her black-sheep reputation in high school. She reasoned that if she was going to be known as the family rebel, she might as well live up to it. She pushed a lot of boundaries and questioned many norms, and she was often in trouble for one reason or another.

She chose to travel for a year after high school before going to college, and even now, all these years later, she knows it was one of the finest decisions she ever made—for the first time in her life, she wasn't living in the shadows of her sisters.

Vicky gets along well with her sisters now that they're grown and have families of their own. Vicky is no longer considered a troublemaker, thanks to a decent profession and an outstanding salary, but a large part of her still feels like she never quite fits in, so she keeps her sisters at arm's length.

Vicky is a social outcast.

The Outcast's Prototype

The Outcast prototype, the typical rugged individualist, is plagued by a fear of rejection or trusting other people—a concern that frequently shows itself by rejecting others before she has a chance to be rejected. The Outcast frequently appears brave to outside onlookers, as if she doesn't care what others say and isn't scared to make her path, speak her mind, think outside the box, and do things differently.

Outcasts, on the other hand, typically retain a basic conviction that other people cannot be relied on or trusted, and they tend to interpret even the slightest insult or dismissal as confirmation of that idea, causing them to reject others even more frequently. Outcasts will anticipate the worst even if the circumstance isn't personal and they aren't being rejected.

Outcasts are frequently anxious to "prove" themselves to the world, whether via remarkable accomplishments, financial success, social position, or extreme conduct since they believe they are undeserving of love and acceptance.

The Outcast is a nonconformist who rejects norms and constraints in favour of doing her own thing. She despises convention and wants to find things out on her own. Again, from the outside, this gives the Outcast the appearance of being brave, but in truth, this "I don't care" attitude is a method of rejecting people before being rejected herself.

When pushed to its logical conclusion, the Outcast character can occasionally lead to self-destructive or illegal conduct. Because Outcasts believe the world is conspiring against them, they have no incentive to "colour inside the lines." As a result, Outcasts might be selfish and egotistical, viewing life exclusively from their own perspective, and they can struggle to demonstrate empathy.

Outcasts struggle to work as part of a team, seek support or assistance from others, or collaborate on group tasks. They can be rude at times, and they like to do things their own way, without interference from others. They like to work on their own.

Outcasts have strong ideas and opinions and are not hesitant to communicate them; in fact, Outcasts may often utilise polarising or controversial comments to push other people away or reject them before they can be rejected.

The Outcast is the fourth most prevalent fear prototype, with

15% of individuals ranking it as their top prototype and 38% ranking it in their top three.

Positive Characteristics

Outcasts are frequently highly successful because they are ambitious, self-motivated, and determined to achieve (even if it is to prove themselves). Their perseverance keeps them continuing when many others give up, and they are also more willing to accept chances than other individuals. While the Outcast is not always a great team player, when not derailed by trust difficulties or divisive remarks, he or she may be a surprisingly excellent leader. The Outcast is not scared to make errors and is skilled at grasping chances and accepting accountability and responsibility.

As an individualist, the Outcast is a skilled critical thinker and may create complicated ideas. Outcasts are drawn to careers that allow them to attain personal success and notoriety while also thinking outside the box. They like to lead rather than follow, and they prefer to accomplish things entirely on their own, which typically leads them to professions in entrepreneurship, business, acting, directing, writing, art, or independent contractors.

Behaviours And Habits

- Tends to believe that others will constantly disappoint them down.
- Is frequently frightened of allowing others to get too close.
- Tends to have just a few extremely intimate connections.
- Prefers to "get deep" in discussion rather than engage in pleasantries.
- Is typically fearless to speak her mind or tell others what she thinks; as a result, she might be perceived as a jerk or a blowhard.
- She frequently feels as though she does not fit in or belong.

- Can be extremely sensitive to any perceived rejection, real or imagined, and is frequently unduly or irrationally outraged when someone cancels plans or fails to include her.
- Occasionally lacks tact or empathy.
- Can be selfish and egotistical; wants everything done her way.
- Has issues with collaboration and teamwork at times.
- Isn't scared to try new ideas or think outside the box.
- Has a dislike for following the crowd.

The Voice Of The Outcast

Here are some of the ideas and views that survey respondents who scored high on the Outcast scale.

• "I'm concerned that I won't be talented enough for my business to thrive and that no one will buy my photography."

• "I hated having to labour for others, which is why I created my own business."

• "I travelled to a different location to meet new individuals. I felt OK at first, but then I became quite restless, anxious, and concerned that others would not like me. I exited the party. After that, I was punishing myself because I had planned to attend, arranged to go, and went, but my fear of being hated got the best of me."

• "I don't want to put myself out there to have the door shut in my face."

• "I'm afraid I'll never be accepted or appreciated for what I've achieved."

• "I'm afraid of getting close to other people. I might meet new friends, but because of my history, I'm too afraid to face my fears and take a leap of faith to trust others."

• "I've learned that I can't rely on anyone and that if I want something done, I have to do it myself."

• "I believe that if you put too much trust in people, they will always let you down."

• "My husband died a year ago, and I recently wanted to

explore online dating but decided against it. I'm just forty years old and don't want to live alone for the rest of my life, but I'm afraid to put myself out there for fear of rejection. I'm disappointed with myself, but not enough to act since I can reason it away."

- "I don't need to blend in with the crowd. I like to pursue my own interests."

How This Fear Can Hold You Back

While outcasts may look fearless—speaking their minds, trying new things, choosing independence, and daring to take risks—their fear of rejection may frequently hold them back in ways that aren't always obvious.

Here are some of the ways that being an outcast may harm you and hold you back:

- You may have a deep-seated notion that others cannot be trusted, which makes you hesitant to open up or expose yourself. This can make it difficult to cultivate deep and lasting relationships, as well as valuable commercial ties.
- You may be too sensitive to any apparent rejection, even if you are not being rejected.
- You may be so motivated to succeed that your success comes at the price of other people and relationships.
- You frequently have difficulty working with and cooperating with others.
- You may take risks or make judgments that are possibly harmful, unhealthy, or unlawful.
- You may push away those who are attempting to assist you.
- When you believe you are being left out, you may experience worry and panic.
- You may lack empathy or a filter at times. This may be interpreted adversely by others, exacerbating your sentiments of rejection.

- You may be stubborn and egotistical, and you tend to want things to go your way all the time.
- You are introverted or antisocial, and you just do not enjoy being in the company of most people.

Methods For Overcoming This Fear

Here are a few methods to help you overcome your fear of rejection if you are an Outcast.

Reframe

As with the majority of the other characteristics, a large part of your fear stems from the script that runs in your head—in this case, the ideas that others cannot be trusted and that it is best to reject others before they reject you.

If you want to overcome your fear, you must reframe the message, write a new screenplay, and generate alternative affirmations that you can repeat to yourself regularly to modify the message that is being played.

For example, if you deeply think that people cannot be trusted, start telling yourself things like, "Just because people have hurt me in the past does not indicate that all people are untrustworthy. There are many individuals in my life that I can rely on." Similarly, if you are afraid that others will reject you or let you down, alter your script to read, "Just because someone says no or disagrees with my concept does not imply they are rejecting me as a person."

TAKE INITIATIVE

Along with changing the narrative that is presently playing in your brain, you will need to practice trusting and working with people in real-life circumstances. This will assist you in confirming and validating your new ideas.

Begin deliberately looking for opportunities to put yourself out there a little more, particularly in circumstances you typically avoid. Perhaps you should ask for assistance when you would typically do it yourself or join a group when your natural tendency is to go it alone. If you have severe trust difficulties, try seeing a counsellor to examine what may be at the root of your fear.

Most importantly, attempt to lower your "rejection" barrier and not automatically think you've been rejected when someone says no. The vast majority of the time, they are not rejecting you!

ESTABLISH ACCOUNTABILITY

As an Outcast, you have difficulty allowing yourself to be vulnerable. It is so critical to actively focus on opening up, even if only to one or two trustworthy accountability partners. This will most likely feel entirely out of the ordinary at first. Nonetheless, seeking responsibility and honest feedback is essential for overcoming anxiety. Your accountability partner will assist you in identifying when your inner Outcast is throwing up your defences and will be able to help you overcome your fear of rejection.

You may also think about hiring a mentor and allowing him or her to advise you. As an Outcast, you may find this especially challenging since you are not accustomed to asking the assistance of others, but doing so will push you outside of your comfort zone in just the manner you need to be pushed. Working with a mentor will not feel natural at first, but with the aid of someone you like and trust, you will ultimately realise the benefits of working collaboratively with another person.

Getting Over Rejection

The first indication that Vicky's perceptions of how her family regarded her were distorted occurred on her 37th birthday. Vicky's sisters and dad came over to celebrate, and after a few glasses of wine, she made a joke about her parents preferring her sisters since she had never really fit in.

Her mother's reaction astounded her.

"Vivi, we have always loved and respected your independence, and we wanted to encourage you, but you always appeared to block us out," she explained. I had to sneak into your room to get your drama schedule and then hide at the back of the auditorium so you wouldn't see me watching since I was worried you didn't want me there."

Then her sisters joined in.

"You were always so much cooler than the rest of us, Vi. We assumed you despised us."

Everything Vicky had thought about herself and her family for years was suddenly cast in a new light, and she knew it was time to alter her worldview.

She sought counsel from one of her closest friends and began to realise how this cycle of pushing people away had been playing out her whole life, fuelled by her fear of rejection.

Vicky was resolved to take action, beginning with her family. She started planning regular "sister evenings," where the three would go out to dinner to talk and reconnect. Vicky couldn't believe how much fun they had together—how much she had missed out on all those years she had kept them at arm's length.

She also tried harder to connect with her coworkers, even summoning the confidence to ask if she might join them for happy hour. She was astounded when they informed her that they believed she disliked them and so never inquired. And, as a result of her new contacts, she learned of professional prospects that she would not have known about otherwise.

Vicky gradually began to let go of her idea that people could not be trusted, allowing herself to be more vulnerable and connected to others. Vicky's feelings are still damaged from time to time, but she is happier and more accepted than she has ever been.

4

Fear Of Making A Mistake

LINDA HAS ALWAYS PREFERRED things to be just right. She is very careful about how she dresses, does her hair, and decorates her home. These things must be done correctly, even if she can't always describe what that means. In fact, she'll spend hours fine-tuning the slightest details—changing her top, shoes, or accessories, or moving a vase or photo frame about the room—just to get everything exactly so.

The need to make things perfect is a recurring topic for Linda. The fact is that the prospect of making a mistake terrifies her, often to the point that she is afraid to start at all. To compensate for this fear, she typically begins working on a project early to allow herself as much time as possible, knowing that she would most likely be adjusting right up to the last minute, wanting to ensure everything is exactly right.

She used to try to get ahead on her studies as a student, sometimes starting before the teacher had even handed out the assignment. Despite this, she never handed in an assignment until the very last minute, often pulling all-nighters just to double-check and modify everything one more time until it was flawless. But if she had a particularly dreadful task, she would put it off practically indefinitely.

Linda now works as a graphic designer for a rapidly expanding start-up coffee company. She likes her job (and the coffee), but she finds it stressful. Because the firm is developing so fast, things are always changing, and it seems that virtually every project she's been asked to work on is needed right away, leaving Linda with little time to prepare. Her boss has no idea that she frequently stays up all night revising her ideas to complete them on time. The lack of sleep, the continual change, and the enormous pressure she places on herself to keep everything perfect begin to wear Linda down.

Change makes Linda exceedingly uncomfortable. She loves to adhere to a schedule and to things she is quite familiar with. Her friends and husband make fun of her for being rigid, but Linda prefers to think of herself as consistent. Even yet, her demand for consistency may be a hindrance at times. She is afraid about saying yes to anything that is too far outside of her comfort zone, even if a part of her wants to break free. She was too scared to commit when her church recently invited her to join in a mission trip to South Africa. "It just feels so far away, and there are so many unknowns!" she said.

Because her work is so stressful, Linda has considered going it alone and becoming a freelance graphic designer. The idea of working from home and setting her own hours appeals to her, but she is also afraid of making a mistake or blunder when it comes to launching her own business. She is so scared of failing that she is unable to take that first step. Sometimes she feels paralysed.

Linda maintains high standards for herself and others around her. He accuses her of being a perfectionist when she and her husband argue. Linda is perplexed as to why this is such a negative thing. What's the harm in wanting everything to be perfect? In her opinion, it is preferable not to do anything at all than to do anything and have it be incorrect.

Linda is a chronic procrastinator.

The Procrastinator's Prototype

The Procrastinator prototype, also known as the Perfectionist, is plagued by the fear of making a mistake, which frequently shows as a fear of commitment or a fear of getting started. Because she is afraid of making a mistake, the Procrastinator seeks for—and frequently finds—any number of perfectly reasonable reasons not to start or attempt at all.

On the surface, the Procrastinator typically shows conduct that appears to be the polar opposite of procrastination, such as planning ahead of time or attempting to work ahead. It is critical to understand that procrastination does not always occur in the classic sense of deferring things until the last minute for the Procrastinator. Instead, the Procrastinator wants to avoid making mistakes; therefore, she will allow herself as much time as possible to complete work.

When it comes down to it, the Procrastinator is frequently reluctant to act and can get immobilised by indecision, especially when definite action must be taken immediately. The Procrastinator prefers to spend an excessive amount of time studying, preparing, or organising. While this degree of preparation can be beneficial, it can also impede progress when study, planning, and organisation become a replacement for action.

Procrastinators, at their heart, are scared of messing up or making a major mistake, especially one that cannot be undone, and this intense fear can keep them from going ahead toward their goals and aspirations. They frequently need an outside force or a deadline to drive them to act; they will occasionally put things off indefinitely if left to their own devices.

According to our poll, the Procrastinator is the most frequent of all fear prototypes, with 41% of respondents ranking it as their top prototype and 74% ranking it among their top three.

Positive Characteristics

The Procrastinator's need for perfection feeds a desire for excellence. She loves perfection and holds herself to a very high standard, which results in high-quality work in general. The Procrastinator excels at jobs that need obsessive attention to detail or excessive thoroughness in preparation. Furthermore, the Procrastinator's diligence in study and preparation leads to fewer errors and a better final product.

Procrastinators like order and structure and are adept at devising systems. They are frequently focused, motivated, and hard-working, with a strong work ethic. They are goal-oriented and task-oriented. A scientific study, engineering, writing and editing, interior design, graphic design, teaching, and administration are among jobs in which the Procrastinator is drawn and excels.

Behaviours And Habits

- Prefers to prepare ahead of time to allow for as much time as feasible.
- Vacations and big projects are sometimes planned months or even years in advance.
- Has strong attention to detail.
- Delays or avoids tasks in which they lack confidence.
- Has a natural need for order and organisation
- Checks and double-checks often to ensure that everything is right.
- There is never a sense that things are "ready."
- Enjoys research and believes that there is always more to learn about a subject.
- Can be highly critical of themselves.
- Becomes unhappy or severely disturbed as a result of errors.
- Is time-conscious and highly aware of deadlines.

The Voice Of The Procrastinator

The remarks participants made to explain their fears were one of the most striking aspects of the survey. Each prototype has its own voice, its distinct manner of portraying how terror seems and feels. All of the statements below are taken from respondents who scored high on the Procrastinator score.

- "I'm so humiliated about not attaining perfection that I can't even begin."
- "I'm constantly concerned that I don't have all of the necessary information to proceed."
- "I hate the sense of being uncomfortable in an unfamiliar setting. When it comes to trying new things, I become apprehensive about change and am constantly terrified of failing."
- "I'm just scared of failure. I'm not sure how I'd manage failure at my "huge goal," and that's what keeps me from starting. I don't want to let my husband and son down if I fail, and I don't want others to judge me based on my failure rather than what I do every day in my current job."
- "I'm scared of failing and, at times, of achieving. Essentially, I believe I am frightened of change, and my inner self holds me back since what I know now is 'safe.'"
- "I'm afraid that I'm going to fail. I'm also hesitant to put myself out there in case I fail. I find it quite unsettling to be put in unfamiliar situations."

How This Fear Can Hold You Back

While the Procrastinator's attention to detail and an almost obsessive dedication to excellence are admirable traits, her underlying fear of making a mistake or committing to an irreversible course of action might limit her ability to take chances, try new things, or commit to large, scary goals.

Here are some of the ways that being a Procrastinator may harm you and hold you back:

- You are so concerned with long-term planning that you fail to capitalise on the current possibilities in front of you.
- You say no much too frequently.
- You are immobilised by the fear of making a mistake, so much so that you are unable to take even the first step.
- You're never quite ready to start, so you don't.

- You spend so much time studying, preparing, and arranging that you never start.
- You have difficulty meeting deadlines.
- You struggle to achieve your own lofty standards and are rarely entirely happy with your work.
- You find it difficult to complete critical undertakings because you believe there is always more tweaking and polishing that might be done.
- You have difficulty giving yourself grace or allowing yourself to attempt new things and make mistakes.
- When you don't have enough time for study and planning, you experience worry and fear.

Methods For Overcoming This Fear

Here are a few ways to help you overcome your fear of making a mistake if you are a Procrastinator.

Reframe

When you begin to see life as a series of lessons rather than mistakes, you will have more flexibility to explore rather than constantly aiming for perfection. The fear of making a mistake or a mistake paralyses the Procrastinator and prevents them from taking any action at all. Of course, if you don't take action, you'll never be able to achieve any of your main goals and aspirations, which is why it's critical to understand how to reframe the way you perceive mistakes or all imperfections and things that go wrong.

TAKE INITIATIVE

One easy but extremely effective adjustment you can make right now is to begin adding more hard deadlines to your calendar—deadlines with repercussions if you don't fulfil them. It might be a self-inflicted penalty, or you could enlist the help of others, such as your spouse, a trusted friend, or even your employer, to set the date and establish the penalty. Just bear in mind that the more "real" the deadlines you can set, the more likely you will be to meet them.

As a Procrastinator, your instinct is to put as much time as possible between yourself and the deadline. Sometimes that means planning too far ahead of time, and other times it means waiting until the last possible moment. In any case, that implies that you need a finish line more than anything else!

Make it a point to practice imperfect action—do one thing every day just for the sake of doing it, not because it has to be "right." For example, you might practice turning in a work assignment as a rough draft rather than the final product, just to see how it feels. In the end, the only antidote to fear is action, which means that the more you practice taking action—even tiny steps in the correct direction—the simpler it will be to take greater steps and more spectacular action.

Establish Accountability

An accountability partner is someone who encourages, supports, and challenges you to follow through on a commitment. Finding an accountability partner who is not a fellow Procrastinator is critical for a Procrastinator. Only someone with different talents and a different fear model than you can give the needed alternate perspective. Look for someone who will push you to take action and keep moving forward even when things aren't ideal and who will call you out when you procrastinate or are scared to commit.

Going Above And Beyond Perfection

Linda understands that she will probably always be someone who loves things "just so," but she has also deliberately begun to take steps to overcome her fear of failing and making mistakes, which have held her stuck.

She began by putting up a sign on her desk that said, "There are no mistakes, only lessons." She's not sure she believes it yet, but she appreciates having the reminder in front of her. And, in the last few weeks, she's observed that the fear and stress she's usually felt immediately before submitting a new assignment has actually decreased substantially.

Linda has also started using a timer to complete certain jobs, in addition to setting strict deadlines for each big assignment. This has allowed her to quit the never-ending tinkering, and she recognises that her work may be better as a consequence. Her boss hasn't seen any difference in quality, but Linda is less worried due to all the adjustments.

While she is beginning to love her work more, Linda's newfound freedom to make errors has encouraged her to consider venturing out on her own as a freelancer. Linda joined a Facebook community for independent graphic artists to give herself encouragement and support. She's made some wonderful contacts and gotten answers to many of her questions regarding freelance life. She took action and followed through when a couple of the designers advised her to approach her boss if he would consider hiring her as a part-time contractor while she built her freelancing business. Her boss, to her surprise, said yes!

Linda had no idea how much her demand for perfection was affecting her life, but she now realises how much her fear of making mistakes was holding her back in so many different ways. Furthermore, she is astounded at how much better and satisfied she feels now that she is actively striving to overcome her fear—even if it means making a mistake occasionally.

5

Fear Of Colouring Outside The Lines

JESSICA HAS ALWAYS KEPT it simple. She was the one who never stepped out of line or questioned her teacher when she was a youngster, so she was responsible and trustworthy. She worked hard. She coloured inside the lines. She strictly adhered to all of the rules. And she'd known she wanted to be a cop since she was a child.

Jessica became a police officer in a community about twenty miles from where she grew up after serving four years in the military. She likes her job for the most part. She loved knowing exactly what was expected of her since the law was plain and straightforward. She put in her time, followed the rules, and rose through the ranks exactly as she was meant to.

Jessica contributed to the community and was an active member of her church in her free time. She and her husband purchased a few acres outside of town, and following the birth of their three children, they began producing their own veggies as a family effort. Jessica's fascination with gardening grew quickly; she enjoyed seeing how the more work she put in — and the more meticulous she was about supplying precisely the correct quantity of water and fertiliser — the better the results she received.

She enjoyed canning and pickling and soon began distributing her homemade salsas and spicy pickles as presents to friends and family. They couldn't get enough of it.

Jessica enjoyed her life because it was stable and predictable.

Then she was injured.

Jessica's accident was unfortunate since it did not occur at work, which would have secured her an early retirement and disability payments. In reality, it was simply a dumb thing. She tripped on a stair while assisting a friend with a move and tore a ligament and some cartilage in her knee. She was taken out of the field and put to temporary desk duties, but that assignment became permanent after her knee failed to recover properly. The move resulted in a demotion and a substantial wage loss.

And Jessica's life was no longer as stable or predictable as it had been. Jessica realised she needed to find a method to supplement her income with three years until she could start receiving her pension, so she started selling her handmade relishes and salsa at the local farmers' market. Jessica excelled at discovering new taste combinations and implementing them into her goods. They were excellent and quite popular, and she quickly gained a local following.

Now, a handful of her most devoted clients are urging her to expand her fledgling business, creating a brand for her items and maybe even selling online. On the other hand, Jessica is afraid to move forward, despite her desire to make more money. She is aware that several rules govern the sale of food, and she is unsure how she would ever fulfil all of them. Selling at a farmers market is one thing —the rules are rather lax—but starting a genuine business, selling online, and maybe even exporting out of state appears to be entirely out of her league. Where can she even begin to look for a comprehensive list of all the requirements? And what if she overlooks something? She is terrified of breaking a big rule or getting into trouble. She feels immobilised every time she even considers the possibility.

There is just no way. And now she's stuck.

Jessica is a Rule Follower.

The Rule Follower's Prototype

Often sticklers for doing things the way they are "supposed" to be done, people who exhibit the Rule Follower pattern are plagued by an irrational fear of authority, which expresses itself as an illogical aversion to violating the rules or doing anything that may be regarded as "not permitted." Even if the prospective "penalty" is just imagined, the Rule Follower is deterred from taking action or going ahead.

Rule Followers perceive the world in black and white and become concerned if they notice themselves or others deviating from the rules of acceptable behaviour. They may be obsessed with ensuring that others make sound judgments and may be regarded as curious at times. The Rule Follower is fundamentally convinced that chaos will result if things are not done according to the rules. Her mindset is that many things in life are simply the way they are and should not be questioned or altered. When she is proven to be accurate or when a decision is proven to be proper, the Rule Follower feels motivated.

Rule Followers frequently disregard their own best judgment in favour of adhering to the rules because their irrational fear of straying outside the lines trumps all else. This fear might also discourage Rule Followers from pursuing their own goals or aspirations. They are frequently reluctant to follow their intuition or to take action that does not feel obvious and transparent. Rule Followers are conformists who can be a little strict. They appreciate knowing that there is a "right" way to do things, and they find comfort in adhering to the established standards. They are uncomfortable with the concept of thinking outside the box or establishing their own path, and they can be critical of those who do not toe the line in the same way they do.

The Rule Follower is the second most prevalent fear prototype, with 14% of individuals ranking it as their top prototype and 64% ranking it in their top three.

Positive Characteristics

The Rule Follower is a reliable, trustworthy friend and coworker. She is extremely attentive, thorough, and steady, caring, and considerate, and she can be depended on to watch out for others.

The Rule Follower has a strong moral code, a clear sense of right and wrong, and great discernment. A dedication to volunteer work or public service exemplifies this sense of responsibility and obligation to individuals and the community at large.

The Rule Follower is extremely rigorous about details and excels in follow-through, always making sure to dot the i's and cross the t's. She takes the time to study the tiny print and ensure she has done her homework. Rule Followers are naturally drawn to careers with very clear guidelines and a well-established, straightforward path to follow, such as police departments, engineering, mathematics, computer programming, public service, law, and medicine because they like knowing that there is a right and wrong way to do things.

Behaviours And Habits

- Desires that things be done the "correct" way and in the "proper" sequence.
- Enjoys knowing that there is a predetermined strategy or process to follow.
- Observes people to ensure they are making sound judgments.
- Tends to perceive the world in black and white.
- Is hesitant to walk outside the lines because he is afraid of getting "in trouble."
- Is a creature of habit; enjoys order and regularity
- Works hard to keep her life stable and predictable.
- Has a strong desire to be correct.
- Eliminates turmoil and ambiguity

The Voice Of The Rule Follower

Some of the ideas and beliefs were revealed by respondents who earned a high Rule Follower score in the fear survey.

- "I'm most concerned about the unknown and undiscovered region where I may not have a support system to guide me."
- "I like it when someone shows me exactly what to do or provides me with a strategy to follow. As long as I know the strategy works, I will stick to it!"
- "It irritates me when people do not follow the rules or do things correctly."
- "I constantly have to make sure that I know all I need to know and that I'm following any rules that regulate what I do."
- "I've spent my entire adult life asking permission. I'm always concerned that what I want to accomplish will be precluded."
- "I struggle with knowing precisely what to do and executing it the 'correct way' the first time."
- "I hate the thought of getting things wrong."
- "I'm more concerned about whether I'm making the 'correct' decision. I frequently wonder, If I choose this choice, what am I losing out on by not picking the other option?"

How This Fear Can Hold You Back

While the Rule Follower has many great and desirable characteristics, the illogical fear of violating the rules, doing something incorrectly, or even getting into trouble may be a major impediment to attempting new things or establishing and attaining big objectives. The Rule Follower will frequently dismiss an alternative before ever considering it, just because doing it the "right" way seems difficult.

Here are some of the ways that being a Rule Follower may harm you and hold you back:

- While you may occasionally fantasise about doing something different, you will frequently avoid taking risks, such as changing jobs, establishing a business, relocating to a new location, or returning to school.

- You may succumb to peer pressure or accept a popular viewpoint because it is the current quo rather than because it suits you.
- You may struggle to extend grace to yourself or accept the opportunity to attempt new things and make mistakes.
- You may struggle to establish a positive connection with nonconformists or those who have demonstrated bad judgment in some aspect of their lives. Because you prefer to perceive things in black and white, you may be inflexible and harsh.
- Your excessive fear of authority may drive you to submit to the demands of someone in a position of power rather than taking a stance or exercising your own judgment.
- When you don't have a clear direction or plan of action, you may experience worry and fear.
- You may let preconceived notions about your own gender, colour, religion, social position, or educational level determine what you feel capable of.

Methods For Overcoming This Fear

Here are a few methods to help you overcome your fear of doing something unethical.

Reframe

It's not always simple to make your own rules, especially when you're most at ease following other people's. Even yet, taking the time to develop and implement your own set of principles—the essential core values you wish to follow in your own life—can help relieve the continual pressure you feel from conforming to everyone else's conventions. Your principles don't have to be complicated or even unique, but they should ring true to you and fit within your existing set of basic values. These will provide you with your own set of principles to follow—guidelines that should take precedence over the "rules" you hear from other people and other sources.

Approach this set of concepts proactively as well as reactively. To begin, make a rough copy of your beliefs to remind yourself of how you like to conduct your life. Second, consider a specific circumstance that challenges you and identify the verbal or unwritten norm you feel obligated to follow. Third, modify the rule to reflect your own beliefs and guidelines for living. In many companies, for example, an unwritten (and unattainable!) "law" is, "Give it your best or you will fail and feel guilty." Change that rule to say, "I will donate X—and no more." And I will not let anyone make me feel bad about donating X. On my terms, I can be successful."

Take Initiative

Make a list of the rules you're afraid of breaking and attack them one at a time. The need to conform to the way things are meant to be might be overpowering for a Rule Follower. When you take the time to write out those rules, you'll discover they aren't actually "rules" at all or that they are easily studied and followed. Not all rules are harmful, but fear of breaking the rules should not be your motivator. Rewrite the story in your brain, and you could find that the rules you were so frightened of breaching aren't as crucial as you believed.

While you're at it, practice "breaking the rules" and venturing outside of your comfort zone in non-risky ways. Daring to speak up when someone is being nasty, rearranging your furniture in new and imaginative ways, or even ignoring the directions if you've never done it before are all examples of pushing your limits. Begin with the little things, and you might be surprised at how much simpler the larger things become! As a Rule Follower, your comfort zone is usually rather well-defined. As a result, starting small will be beneficial if you want to get more comfortable with doing difficult things, taking chances, and daring to act in the face of fear.

Establish Accountability

You will need to locate an accountability partner who is not a Rule Follower if you are a Rule Follower. Instead, seek someone with different talents, a different attitude, or a different fear prototype than you and may offer a new perspective on the rules you feel obligated to obey. Find someone who pushes you to utilise your own judgment and critical thinking abilities rather than reverting to the way things are "supposed to be"—someone who will hold you responsible when viewing a situation in black-and-white terms.

Getting Over The Fear Of Breaking The Rules

One of Jessica's greatest customers, Jane, mentioned again at the farmers market one Saturday morning that she wished Jessica would take her company to the next level and start selling online.

"Jessica, your tastes are fantastic! The world requires your salsa!"

Jessica smiled, sighed, and sadly remarked, "I simply don't know how I'd get past all those laws and regulations. I'm so terrified of making a mistake that I don't know where to begin."

Jane, on the other hand, was taken aback by her reaction this time. "Well, why don't you go take a class or get some assistance with the regulations? I'm sure there must be some kind of conference or training for this. You should investigate!"

Jessica was astounded. Why hadn't she thought of that before? She started conducting research as soon as she came home from the market and discovered an e-commerce conference was taking place the next month in a city about three hours away. She registered for the conference right away, crossing her fingers that she was doing the right thing.

Jessica's decision turned out to be the finest she'd ever made. She registered for the food-sellers track at the conference, where she took a seminar on how to negotiate food safety standards and regulations. She had all of her major concerns addressed, and she came away with a clear plan of action for what to do next. But that wasn't the end of it. She also established some fantastic contacts with other retailers who had been selling online for a while and learned a ton about other parts of e-commerce that had previously frightened her, such as how to construct a website and how to handle sales and marketing. While she was there, she joined an online coaching group that would give her guidance and support along the journey.

Jessica felt empowered to pursue her ambition now that she had a set of "instructions" to follow. She stuck to every step of the strategy that had been laid out for her, and within a few months, she had put up her website and was selling online.

Jessica is enthusiastic about the unknown for the first time in her life, rather than terrified of it. Face-to-face with her fears has given her greater confidence, and she can't wait to see what the future holds.

6

Fear Of What Other People Will Think

EVERYBODY LOVES NANCY. She's simply... so... lovely. Thoughtful, compassionate, and generous, and always eager to provide a helping hand. She seldom says no since she dislikes disappointed or disappointing others.

Unfortunately, it is a feature that renders her vulnerable at times. Everyone knows Nancy is the greatest person to ask when they need help or a favour, whether she's at work, church, or even the PTA since she always goes above and beyond the call of duty. Nancy's friends sometimes wonder how she manages to sleep at all. Nancy works at a major construction business as an office manager, and her employer adores her. Why shouldn't he? She is the model employee, arriving early and working late, always ensuring she has done her best, and sometimes even covering for coworkers who haven't quite measured up.

Nancy despises confrontation and tension; therefore, she spends a lot of time attempting to smooth things over and ensure that no one is unhappy or angry. Her employer teases her and refers to her as Pollyanna since she is always trying to see the bright side of things. Nancy has been like this since she was a child. She was raised in a pretty happy family. They were nearly picture-perfect: a mother and father with two children, a girl, and a boy, living in the suburbs in a nice split-level home. But Nancy's elder brother began to rebel in primary school, and by high school, he appeared to be always in trouble. The conflicts at home were epic, and Nancy spent most of her time trying to be the perfect daughter while keeping the stress at bay.

Nancy is very concerned with how she looks and what she wears since she is always worried about what other people would think. She enjoys keeping up with trends but does not want to be too cutting edge. She also takes great delight in designing and caring for her home—she never wants anybody to believe she isn't a good housekeeper!

Nancy has always had a thriving social life and a large circle of friends. She's a lot of fun to be around, and her grin truly brightens up a room. Nancy and her husband get along fine most of the time, primarily because Nancy hates arguing and would generally simply go along with what he wants rather than fighting for her own way. Nancy fantasises about establishing her own business—she'd love to operate a little coffee shop in town—but she has no clue where she'd find the time. Furthermore, she can't face the notion of what people could say, especially if the firm fails. She'd be embarrassed.

Nancy's life can be stressful at times. She spends so much time making everyone else happy that she doesn't have much time to think about her own aspirations and dreams. To be honest, she's not sure what she wants.

Nancy is a People Pleaser.

The People Pleaser Prototype

The People Pleaser prototype is naturally inclined to seek the favour of others, but it suffers most from the fear of being judged, which also shows as the fear of letting people down and the worry of what other people could think. Essentially, the People Pleaser's main concern is frequently summed up as apprehension about how others will react. Because the People Pleaser is so terrified of being judged —or, worse, criticised or ridiculed—and because the People Pleaser is intensely aware of and fearful of how others will respond or what they will say, she might be hesitant to go forward, paralysed with uncertainty, and feel helpless to take action. Above all, she dislikes the prospect of making a fool of herself.

People Pleasers are typically popular and well-liked, even if they do not consider themselves extroverts. Because they are hyperaware of how they may be viewed, they tend to select their words carefully or, in some cases, even conceal their actual opinions about a subject if they appear to contradict the prevailing consensus.

That said, the People Pleaser may frequently be gregarious, humorous, and engaging—the party's life—as a method of gaining acceptance and being liked by others. She may also be preoccupied with status symbols such as a good automobile, a well-appointed home, and designer labels and putting a lot of work into her looks.

The People Pleaser may develop the habit of becoming a "yes woman"—a person who constantly agrees and may even change her own opinions to agree with someone else. She prefers to get along with others and is hesitant to do anything that could elicit resentment, disappointment, or wounded emotions.

People Pleasers might be too concerned with what other people think, making them vulnerable to peer pressure. They have a strong desire to blend in and be accepted. While not always meek, the People Pleaser has difficulty saying no, setting limits, and creating appropriate boundaries because she is scared of disappointing others. Others perceive her as a "giver," or someone helpful, kind, and generous with her time and energy.

While these traits can be beneficial, they can also lead to People Pleasers becoming overcommitted or allowing other people's demands and desires to take precedence over their own goals and ambitions. This might cause deep sentiments of anger or bitterness to rise to the surface in unexpected ways.

The People Pleaser is the third most prevalent fear prototype, with 21% of people ranking it as their top prototype and 63% ranking it in their top three.

Positive Characteristics

People Pleasers are generally the nicest, most considerate, and most generous individuals you'll ever meet. They are considerate and go out of their way to assist. They are popular and well-liked, and they are frequently humorous, pleasant, and engaging. People Pleasers are excellent people to have as friends because of this. They are excellent allies and employees that are dependable, competent, and well-spoken. People Pleasers may fit into virtually any professional path, but they excel in support roles or occupations that need them to interact with others. Administration, nursing, education, social work, customer service, and retail are all common vocations.

Behaviours And Habits

- Is too worried about seeming dumb, ignorant, or ridiculous.
- Never wants to let anyone down.
- Worries excessively about what other people may think or say.
- Has a reputation for being popular and well-liked.
- Is excessively preoccupied with external appearance and status symbols; enjoys "dressing to impress."
- Hides or alters own ideas to fit in; dislikes going against a common opinion or broad agreement.
- Fears losing friendships or being criticised; avoids anything that could jeopardise a friendship.
- Says yes too frequently, which can lead to overcommitment.
- Is concerned about what other people think.
- Is frequently seen as amusing, warm, generous, and kind.
- Has a strong desire to fit in and be accepted by the crowd.

The Voice Of The People Pleaser

Here are some of the ideas and beliefs revealed by our fear study participants who scored highly on the People Pleaser scale.

- "I'm terrified of failing and being mocked or laughed at. I'm afraid I'll lose my friends."

- "I know I shouldn't be, but I'm frightened of what other people think of me and what I'm doing. I'm afraid they won't approve."
- "I'm frightened of seeming dumb, of making others believe I'm squandering money, and of disappointing or making angry those I care about."
- "I'm afraid of being overwhelmed and then disappointing others. I enjoy learning new things, but I become scared when someone else is relying on me. I've let people down in the past due to a lack of time, stamina, or motivation, and it makes me suspicious of my limitations. That is why I frequently undershoot or refuse opportunities."
- "I'm always worried about what other people will say and how they will react."
- "I scheduled a few seminars to speak on health, self-love and overcoming emotional eating, and then I cancelled them all. I allowed my fear of being seen and evaluated as unqualified to prevent me from proceeding."
- "I'm afraid of falling flat on my face in front of other people or seeming to be a fake. I'm concerned about standing out among my peers and performing worse than my colleagues who have advanced to the status of 'professional.'"
- "I'm concerned about making mistakes and failing others." I don't want to make myself seem bad."

How This Fear Can Hold You Back

As a People Pleaser, you risk letting others' views, opinions, and needs to keep you from following your ambitions, interests, and goals.

Here are some of the ways that being a People Pleaser may harm you and hold you back:

- You may postpone taking action or pursuing a goal because you are concerned about what others may think or say about you.
- You may be prone to peer pressure or agreeing with a

popular concept or position just because it appears to be what everyone else is doing and you want to fit in.
- You may find it difficult to say no to requests, leaving you overcommitted and with little time to pursue your own goals and aspirations.
- You may be prone to allowing others to take advantage of your generosity and kindness or to allow them to "walk all over you."
- Your unreasonable fear of disappointing others may drive you to give in to their requests rather than take a stance or apply your judgment.
- You may feel anxious and afraid if you believe you are being judged or have the potential to be judged in some way.
- You may be more concerned with being liked and receiving acceptance from others than with achieving your own goals and aspirations.

Methods for Overcoming This Fear

Here are a few methods to help you overcome your fear of being judged or disappointing others.

Reframe

A large portion of your fear of being judged or of disappointing others stems from the script that plays in your head—a script that suggests others might not love or accept you if you don't act the way you believe they want you to. If you wish to be rid of this fear, you must begin to change the voice in your brain. Create some fresh affirmations that you may repeat to yourself regularly to modify the message that is playing.

If you have a profound fear that others will criticise you or dislike you for saying no, your new affirmation maybe something like, "It's acceptable to have my viewpoint and for other people to disagree." Disagreement does not imply that they dislike me." Similarly, if you are afraid that people will be disappointed with you, tell yourself, "The people who matter are not upset when I establish boundaries." Sometimes it's only a question of changing the script that's already running.

Take Initiative

The essential thing for the People Pleaser to practice is saying no! After all, if you refuse to say no, it won't be long until you're unable to offer your best to anybody or anything. Worse, you'll come to hate the tasks you've taken on, as well as the rest of the things in your life that you should and could be doing if you had just said no. Overcommitment is a negative cycle that may be prevented by simply saying no. Of course, this is easier said than done for a People Pleaser! However, like with anything else in life, the more you practice, the better you will become. So do whatever it takes to improve your skills, whether it's asking for more time to decide, delegating the work to someone else, or having someone say no on your behalf. But, please, say no. Once more, and again, and again.

At the same time, allow yourself to exercise self-care and make time for your own goals, ambitions, and priorities. Make time in your calendar exclusively for yourself. You may have to start small at first, and it may take some time for others to adjust, but remember that when you care for your own needs, you are making yourself better for others.

As a People Pleaser, you've probably spent a long time putting other people's needs before your own, and ignoring your self-care may be wearing you down. However, much like with air masks on a flight, where the rule is to put on your own mask before aiding others, it is critical to take care of yourself to be there for others.

Establish Accountability

Finding a teacher or mentor who represents the characteristics and abilities you want to acquire and allowing her to assist you is one of the finest things you can do to overcome any sort of fear. Find someone with a different fear prototype, such as an Outcast, to help balance out your People Pleasing instincts.

Ideally, it would help if you locate someone prepared to push you beyond your comfort zone—someone who will also help you practice saying no and taking care of yourself. It may seem awkward at first, but you can get there, especially with the aid of someone you like and trust.

Getting Over The Need To Please

Nancy was on the edge of a mental breakdown, but she was too frightened to tell anybody for fear of disappointing them. She was aware that something had to give. She was exhausted from doing too much and not getting enough sleep as she attempted to keep up with all of her responsibilities. Then she got sick with the flu, which pushed her over the edge. She couldn't get out of bed, so she listened to a podcast about self-care and saying no until she realised it was time to make some changes.

Nancy began by talking to her husband, who was relieved to hear that she would start creating more time for herself. He promised her he would love her no matter what, even if she didn't always agree with him.

That meant a lot to Nancy. She then began to say no, politely withdrawing from a few obligations she had previously accepted. She was taken aback when everyone she spoke to appeared to get it, and no one was upset. She understood that the strain she was putting on herself was largely mental. At work, she ceased attempting to resolve every disagreement and instead encouraged team members to resolve issues among themselves. She also began to be more cautious about setting boundaries in terms of her schedule.

But the most significant change for Nancy has been a shift in mindset and the fact that she has permitted herself to prioritise her own needs. She hasn't quite built up the confidence to open her coffee shop yet, but she's getting there.

7

Fear Of Not Being Good Enough

REBECCA HAS ALWAYS WANTED to know what it's like to be self-assured. Sometimes she looks at her three siblings, who appear to have all the confidence in the world, and wishes she could just have a slight amount of whatever they have. They have fulfilling professions, appear to travel frequently, and enjoy life to the fullest, but Rebecca feels as if she is merely watching from the sidelines. It's difficult not to be a bit resentful. It hasn't always been like this, at least not entirely. She was an athlete in high school, the star of the volleyball team. She was named Player of the Year three years in a row.

Despite this, she never felt like she was good enough. She was worried that people would eventually realise she wasn't as good as everyone believed she was. In reality, the true reason she practised so much—almost nonstop—was because she was constantly afraid of falling short and failing to meet everyone else's expectations. She was given a scholarship to play volleyball at University, but she declined, choosing instead for a local team in her spare time. She couldn't take the stress any longer.

But even after all these years, she still wonders, What if...?

After graduation, Rebecca obtained a position as an executive assistant to the top sales manager at a small start-up. While it was difficult at first, and she spent the first year or so scared of making a mistake and being fired, she ultimately learned to enjoy it. It was a lot of fun since she always knew what to do and how to handle any scenario. She did, however, marry and became pregnant shortly after. She resigned from her job; she liked to become a stay-at-home parent at her husband's suggestion. Her three children are now older and more self-sufficient, and while she loves them more than life itself, a part of her has always felt a little angry about giving up her profession.

Rebecca adores her husband, but she occasionally mocks the way he looks and styles his hair, and she frequently remarks that he works too hard and has gained a few pounds in recent years. He believes she is overly critical, and when they argue, he tells her so. Rebecca is aware that she should refrain from criticising others, but she just can't stop herself. Rage seems like it boils up inside her at times, but she understands it has more to do with her dissatisfaction than with anybody else. The truth is that Rebecca's husband isn't the only one who has gained weight. She knows she should, but she can't seem to control her eating.

Rebecca doesn't have many close companions, and she often pines for those women who do. Nonetheless, she can't bring herself to open up in that way. Her husband just struck up a relationship with a coworker, and his wife, Darcy, attempted to befriend Rebecca as well. Rebecca made excuses every time Darcy reached out to her after they had dinner together once.

The fact was that Darcy terrified Rebecca. She was stunning, in excellent condition, owned her training business, could cook like a gourmet chef, and seemed to win friends wherever she went. She was everything Rebecca wished she could be but couldn't.

As a result, rather than confiding in her, Rebecca became increasingly critical of Darcy, frequently making nasty comments to her husband about the way she dressed, her parenting style, and everything else she could think of. When Darcy and her husband chose to leave, the two couples reconnected in a restaurant, where Rebecca finally let down her guard and had a genuine heart-to-heart conversation with Darcy. Rebecca only realised afterwards that her uncertainty had caused her to lose out on what could have been a fantastic friendship.

Rebecca is a Self-Doubter.

The Self-Doubter Prototype

The Self-Doubter, who is often plagued by a deep, sometimes hidden sense of insecurity, struggles most with the fear of not being capable, which frequently manifests itself as the fear of not being good enough, whether "good" means smart enough, naturally gifted enough, educated enough, pretty enough, strong enough, very well, cool enough, or any other number of enough.

Because Self-Doubters are constantly concerned about their qualifications or abilities, they might become paralysed by insecurity and doubt to the point of being unable or reluctant to take any action at all. A voice continuously plagues the Self-Doubter in her brain that says things such as, "You can't do this, You're not capable," or "What makes you think you can do anything like that?" This voice drives the Self-Doubter to continuously doubt her value and to belittle herself.

Self-Doubters, interestingly, sometimes try to disguise or compensate for their insecurity by being too critical and judgemental of others. They transfer their feelings of unworthiness onto others around them, especially those closest to them, who may be taking chances, pursuing their goals and aspirations, or putting themselves out there in some manner. As a result, Self-Doubters might come across as snarky or sarcastic at times.

Self-Doubters may also experience strong envy toward those who are doing things they wish they could accomplish if they weren't so frightened of not being capable. Again, envy may show itself through sarcasm, gossip, or criticism.

This tendency toward jealously and criticism, which stems from a sense of unworthiness, may hurt relationships. Others close to the Self-Doubter may feel as if they can never live up to the Self-standards, Doubter's causing them to withdraw. This, in turn, promotes the Self-perception of Doubter's that she is unworthy.

It's a never-ending loop.

Because the Self-Doubter is deeply insecure, she is frequently, if not always, insatiably hungry for praise and reassurance. The Self-Doubter seeks validation and requires regular words of affirmation to boost her self-esteem.

The Self-Doubter is the fifth most frequent fear prototype, with 3% of respondents ranking it as their top prototype and 24% ranking it in their top three.

Positive Characteristics

The Self-Doubter can be humble, self-effacing, and unpretentious. She is not typically boastful or proud, and she does not have an inflated ego. The Self-Doubter is frequently an incredibly hard worker, constantly prepared to go above and beyond to compensate for any inwardly perceived flaws.

The Self-Doubter is extremely sensitive, and while she might come across as judgmental at times, she is typically compassionate and kind and very concerned with how others feel. The Self-Doubter is attracted to professions with a clear set of instructions and expectations or vocations that allow for mastery of a particular specialised activity.

Behaviours And Habits

- Has a strong fear of not being capable and regularly feels inadequate.
- Has issues with negative self-talk—a voice in the back of her brain that causes her to doubt her value.
- Frequently feels unqualified and "insufficient"—not clever enough, educated enough, beautiful enough, organised enough, and so on.
- Has a propensity to be too critical of herself and others.
- Can appear negative or snarky.
- Has sentiments of envy, especially toward others who are doing something she wishes she could accomplish.
- Requires reassurance and confirmation.

- Humble and self-effacing; does not battle with a big ego.
- Has trouble forming or maintaining friendships at times.
- Is frequently a very hard worker.
- Can feel paralysed or trapped as a result of insecurity
- When asked to do anything new, thinks, Oh, I wouldn't know how to do it.
- Believes that other people are more deserving of achievement than she is.
- Wishes for something better but does not feel she is capable of making the necessary changes.

The Voice Of The Self-Doubter

Here are some of the thoughts and suggestions revealed by survey respondents who scored high on the Self-Doubter scale:

• "I don't set goals because I don't know what I want because I've spent my entire life learning to fit in. The words of my mother and ex-husband play over and over in my head that I'm not good enough and I'll never be good at anything."

• "I let fear keep me from serving as a church leader. I listened to the whispers in my brain tell me I wasn't good enough, that I didn't have enough time, that I didn't know enough about God to teach others, and that people would see straight through me. I allowed myself to overthink everything and punished myself. I backed out and then had to cope with the guilt of disappointing others."

• "I'm afraid I'll fail because I usually do. I keep going until it becomes too difficult, and then I stop. So why even try?"

• "I dislike public speaking and any form of public attention. I've been invited to speak on occasion but have felt unqualified and inadequate. But, after opting not to push me beyond my comfort zone, I felt humiliated and disappointed in myself."

• "I'm so certain I'm going to fail that I don't bother. Plus, I'm sure other people would be perplexed as to why I even attempted when it was apparent I wouldn't succeed."

• "I'm frightened of realising I'm not capable of doing what I truly want to accomplish and that no one will take me seriously or care about what I have to contribute."

- "I know I'm an athlete inside, but I can't seem to act on it. It irritates me and makes me so sad. I want to just go out and do it, but I can't seem to get over that impenetrable barrier."
- "Everyone in my family is so intelligent, and I feel like the idiot who always makes mistakes and never learns from them."
- "I'm terrified of seeming stupid or inept, and I constantly feel that I don't deserve the success or position that I have and that I'll be revealed as an imposter."
- "I was terrified for long years of quitting a career that was depleting me. I didn't believe I could do anything else since I didn't feel successful at my job. Instead of just rejecting the position as maybe not being a good fit, I assumed something was wrong with me. It held me trapped for a very long time."

How This Fear Can Hold You Back?

As a Self-Doubter, you are plagued by a small voice in the back of your brain that leads you to question your own skills by telling you that you are insufficient.

Here are some of the ways that being a Self-Doubter may harm you and keep you back:

- You frequently avoid taking chances or attempting new things because you are concerned that you will not be successful.
- You may find yourself often second-guessing your decisions or changing your mind because you are afraid you won't achieve them.
- Rather than feeling pleased for them, you often feel unhappy or envious when you watch other people succeeding, especially when they succeed at something you want to accomplish but haven't dared to try.
- You may compromise your relationships by being too critical of those closest to you, making them feel they can never come up to your standards.
- Because you don't feel worthy or capable of speaking up,

you may be prone to peer pressure or agreeing with a popular opinion.
- You may struggle with giving yourself or others grace, and you may find it difficult to allow yourself to attempt new things and make mistakes.
- You may experience anxiety and worry if you are forced to take a risk or go outside your comfort zone and do not believe you have enough of the necessary abilities.
- You may let your limiting ideas about your ability determine what you allow yourself to do and what you believe you are capable of.

Methods For Overcoming This Fear

Here are a few techniques to help you overcome your fear of not being good enough.

Reframe

As a Self-Doubter, you may feel bad about yourself when things don't go as planned, when you make a mistake, or when you fail. However, it is critical to realise that mistakes and failure are a natural part of life. Furthermore, it is frequently our errors that teach us everything we need to know to keep going forward!

Is that to say it's enjoyable to make mistakes or have things go wrong? No, of course not, and clearly, the aim is for everything to go smoothly. But you can't allow failure to stop you from going for it or attempting new things because errors and failures are different sorts of victory.

When you deliberate to stop thinking about all the ways you may mess up and instead focus solely on what you can learn from the experience, you give yourself the ability to just attempt, regardless of the outcome. It removes all of the pressure to get it right the first time and instead allows you to truly enjoy the trip.

TAKE INITIATIVE

Action is the cure to fear, and the only way to completely overcome doubts and concerns of not being competent is to begin demonstrating to yourself that you are capable. The good news is that by taking little chances and small steps outside of your comfort zone, you will ultimately get the confidence to take greater risks and larger steps outside of your comfort zone. Nothing builds confidence quicker than taking action while being afraid. So keep practising, and do at least one scary thing every day.

CREATE ACCOUNTABILITY

For the Self-Doubter, the tiny voice inside your mind telling you that you're not capable of succeeding can grow so loud that it drowns out any counter-argument. When this happens, it's easy to become engrossed in your own world of fear and inadequacy, even if those ideas aren't founded in fact. If you're having trouble dealing with self-defeating ideas and emotions of not being good enough, seek reinforcements in the form of an outside view from a trusted friend, mentor, counsellor, or coach.

Of course, this will make you vulnerable, and for the Self-Doubter, this might be the most difficult aspect of all. Even yet, having someone else inform you that your views may be incorrect may make a significant impact. More significantly, a good coach or mentor can show you how to overcome your fears and insecurities.

Getting Over Insecurity

Rebecca's profound regret about her Darcy experience eventually convinced her that she needed to find a method to overcome her severe self-doubt before it ruined her. She began by reading a few self-help books and listening to motivational podcasts, and while these were useful and somewhat inspirational, she recognised she might need some assistance in overcoming the insecurity that had been welling up inside of her for so long.

She scheduled an appointment with a life coach she discovered online since she was uncomfortable talking to anybody she knew directly. Her coach urged her to begin by being more deliberate about practising self-care and doing a few things just for herself, such as joining a recreational volleyball league, acquiring a gym membership, working out with a personal trainer, and joining a recreational volleyball league. Rebecca was surprised at how much fun she had playing volleyball again, especially now that she wasn't under pressure to be the greatest. As she grew more active and in better condition, she began to feel more confident in her looks, which made her feel a lot happier.

People noticed the difference, notably Rebecca's husband and children. Rebecca's life coach also urged her to step outside of her comfort zone and consider returning to work. Rebecca had to muster up the confidence to start searching for jobs for almost six months before she found a fantastic part-time admin position that was both demanding and flexible.

Rebecca's newfound connections, though, mattered the most to her. Instead of feeling envious and unworthy in the presence of other women, she learned to perceive their positive characteristics, and she realised she could enjoy the qualities in others without feeling inadequate about herself.

It was a significant adjustment, and it made all the difference.

8

Fear Of Taking Responsibility

AMANDA IS one of those people who always makes a good first impression. She is someone that others respect and look up to because she is smart, confident, and eloquent. It also helps that she always appears to be quite knowledgeable—she is well-read and can frequently explain the idea or philosophy behind any number of thought leaders in her area.

In fact, Amanda is so adept at expressing other people's views that no one notices when she is cautious not to reveal her thoughts and beliefs or say anything that may be used against her later. Amanda has learned that it is better to hide behind other people's ideas than to offer her own and risk being blamed if they fail. Because she hates being forced.

Amanda's parents had incredibly high expectations of her as she grew up, and they put a lot of pressure on her to obtain good grades and thrive in music and athletics.

They also made a lot of excuses when she didn't live up to their expectations. They phoned her instructors several times to have her grade altered if she did poorly on a test or report, even if the reason she did poorly was that she hadn't studied. They maintained that she didn't make the all-county orchestra because they couldn't afford individual lessons with the director, not because she didn't perform well on her audition.

Amanda learned that as long as she could justify why she fell short, her parents would not be disappointed in her.

Amanda learned early on in college that the secret to getting excellent grades in any subject was learning how to reflect the tutor's views and beliefs. She became quite adept at remembering how to repeat the same words and phrases used during lectures on her examinations. As a result, she was always well-liked, and she received straight A's most of the time.

However, once in a while, a tutor would catch on to her technique and push her to explain her own thoughts. Amanda suffered a lot during that period, to the point where she left the class to avoid being pinned down. Amanda was recruited as a project manager in the corporate office of a big manufacturing business after graduation. She soon developed a name for herself within her department and was regularly promoted over the following few years, finally being named vice president of operations.

Amanda began to suffer in that job, at the top of her department. Until that moment, she had always been invited to weigh in on matters, but the ultimate decision was nearly always taken by someone else. She never had to be concerned about being blamed for a bad judgment or being called out for making the incorrect decision.

She hated being held accountable. It is the reason she finally chose to leave her corporate position to become a consultant. She discovered she enjoyed offering advice, recognising choices, and presenting various perspectives and thoughts to explore without having to make the ultimate decision. She enjoyed keeping up with what was going on in the industry, but she never wanted to be the one to blame.

This propensity has shown itself in her personal life as well. She never wants to be the one to decide her marriage or her friendships, whether it's about which house to purchase or which movie to watch. When she and her husband argue, his most common criticism is that she always has an explanation for everything.

Amanda is an Excuse Maker.

The Excuse Maker's Prototype

The Excuse Maker prototype, also known as the Blame Shifter, suffers most from the fear of taking responsibility, which may also appear as the fear of being held accountable or being discovered at fault. Because the Excuse Maker is afraid of having the finger pointed at her, she is constantly on the lookout for an excuse—someone or something to blame—for why she can't accomplish anything or why her circumstances are what they are.

Often, these justifications and rationalisations appear to be reasonable, making it difficult to pinpoint that the Excuse Maker is transferring blame and avoiding accountability. The Excuse Maker is highly skilled at deflecting attention and emphasis away from herself and her own guilt to other people or events. She is a skilled rationaliser, always having a reason or explanation for why she couldn't do anything.

The Excuse Maker may feel uncomfortable in a leadership capacity and may get anxious at the prospect of being in control, taking chances, or placing herself in danger, preferring instead to submit to the judgment of others. When it comes to making changes in her life or pursuing goals, the Excuse Maker likes to follow the example or advice of others, such as a mentor, coach, or teacher. She pays close attention to what has worked for others and attempts to replicate their success.

The Excuse Maker becomes uneasy when she is put in the position or asked to express her views or ideas for fear of being held accountable or blamed for a negative outcome. Indeed, she will frequently delay sharing her own ideas until others have offered theirs, and she will frequently defer to someone else's judgment rather than taking her own stand.

Ironically, the Excuse Maker prototype's fundamental nature—the inclination to avoid taking responsibility or to make excuses—makes it one of the most difficult prototypes to embrace and accept since its natural tendency is to create explanations that deflect accountability. That is why it is critical to remember that the Excuse Maker prototype is not superior or inferior to the other fear prototypes. The fact is that none of the prototypes is positive; rather, they all impede our progress in some manner. Furthermore, we all have a tiny piece of every one of the prototypes at work within us.

The Excuse Maker is the sixth most prevalent fear prototype, with 3% of individuals ranking it as their top prototype and 20% ranking it in their top three.

Positive Characteristics

Excuse Makers can be terrific team players who excel at communicating and working with others. They are skilled at absorbing lessons from the achievements and failures of others since they are outstanding learners and students of life. They also respond well to guidance, and when partnered with the appropriate mentor or teacher, they may achieve extraordinary results.

Excuse Makers are excellent cheerleaders who are frequently highly supportive of others. They can make others feel and think that they are capable of great things. They are also great observers with excellent insight, even though they occasionally hesitate to express their strong opinions. Excuse Makers thrive and feel most at ease in strong supporting positions rather than direct leadership responsibilities. They flourish in jobs where they can eventually submit to the judgment or opinion of someone in authority.

Behaviours And Habits

- Has difficulty accepting blame or accepting responsibility for a mistake or error.
- Frequently feels that her setbacks and failures result from events beyond her control or of others failing to do their part.
- When anything goes wrong, he or she usually has an excuse or an explanation; this excuse or explanation frequently looks entirely reasonable and sensible, and hence is difficult to identify as an excuse.
- Is hesitant to express her own views for fear of being pinned down or held accountable for it.

- Feels hampered by a lack of guidance, support, or leadership, either now or in the past (i.e., bad parents, teachers, bosses, etc.)
- Sometimes connects present difficulties to events that occurred a long time ago or in her adolescence.
- Requires the assistance of a teacher or guide to show her the way.
- Difficulties making choices in a group environment or on behalf of others.
- Rather than going out on her own, she prefers to cooperate and interact with others.

The Voice Of The Excuse Maker

Here are some of the thoughts and perspectives revealed by survey participants who earned a high Excuse Maker score:

- "Money is really tight right now, which is preventing me from going forward with what I want to accomplish."
- "I'm afraid that if something goes wrong, everyone will be upset with me, and I'll be blamed."
- "I've always wanted to run my own small bakery, but I don't have the financial means to do so. Student loans make up a significant portion of our debt, and I don't see this dream coming true."
- "I am frequently overwhelmed by how much there is to study and how little time I have before my payments are due. I need to start earning money right away, not in six months."
- "I don't want to be the one who is accountable to everyone else."
- "I don't think I should do it since I don't have the time or resources to accomplish it well."
- "My greatest ambition in life is to be a horse trainer, but with minimal equestrian experience at the age of twenty-two, I believe I'm too old to start my career in that field. All of the successful horse trainers appear to have started before they could even walk. The concept is quite intimidating to me, and it appears to be impossible."
- "I'd want to establish my own business, but it seems that

someone or something constantly gets in the way. I don't have the time. I don't have any money. There is no one to instruct me."

- "I've always wanted to write a book. I've always wanted to be a writer, but I never do. I'm always coming up with an excuse. I know it's because I'm scared, but I'm not sure how to go over it."

- "I'm terrified of having to do it alone, with no support system and no one to depend on."

How This Fear Can Hold You Back

The most serious threat to the Excuse Maker prototype is her refusal to accept complete responsibility for her life, and all that occurs to her. This natural propensity to avoid being criticised or held responsible and instead create excuses is a way to relinquish control of her future. Because, in the end, even the best reason is still an excuse.

Here are some of the ways being an Excuse Maker may harm you and keep you back:

- You may struggle to reach a final choice or conclusion if it is not one reached first by someone else.
- It may be difficult for you to express your own views and opinions for fear of being held accountable for them afterwards.
- Taking the initiative may make you feel uneasy if it implies that you will be held accountable or blamed if things go wrong.
- You are skilled at making good excuses or rationalisations for why you shouldn't try something or why you weren't able to do something, even if those reasons aren't helping you in the long run.
- Your inclination to make excuses or transfer blame can be annoying to others when it appears that you are hesitant to accept responsibility for your mistakes; this can hurt your relationships.
- When you feel held down, blamed, or expected to accept responsibility for a choice, you may experience

anxiety, wrath, or fear, and you may react by lashing out.
- You may find it difficult to take chances.
- You may be prone to attributing current difficulties or setbacks to events in the past, such as a difficult upbringing, a lack of support, or a lack of a great mentor. This keeps you from fully accepting responsibility at the moment.

Methods For Overcoming This Fear

Here are a few ways to help you overcome your fear of assuming responsibility.

Reframe

A large portion of your fear stems from the screenplay that has been playing in your head—the message that says you don't want to bear the blame. As a result, changing your perspective on accepting ownership and accountability will assist you in moving forward.

If you truly feel that making excuses will keep you from being blamed, try telling yourself, "No one loves to hear excuses. When I accept responsibility for my work, people are far more inclined to value it." Similarly, if you're dealing with events beyond your control, tell yourself, "I may not have control over everything, but I can accept responsibility for the decisions I make."

TAKE INITIATIVE

As an Excuse Maker, you may discover that adopting a no-excuses attitude is the most effective move you can do in your life. When you decide to accept responsibility for every choice and decision you make, you are displaying bravery. A no-excused mindset implies putting a stop to all reasons and refusing to blame someone who has hurt you, your current circumstances, or the awful things that have occurred to you.

Psychologists refer to this as a change in the locus of control, which is the degree to which individuals think they have internal control over their lives instead of believing that external factors beyond their control govern their lives. People with an internal centre of control are, predictably, considerably more driven, productive and successful in life. As a result, becoming more driven is frequently a question of accepting responsibility for your actions.

While it may appear frightening at first, it is extremely liberating to adopt a no-excuses mindset and accept total responsibility for your life and circumstances! When you take ownership, you don't have to worry about what happens to you, how other people treat you, or what obstacles may arise since you are ultimately in control.

ESTABLISH ACCOUNTABILITY

It's never easy to have someone else point out your own tendency to make excuses, but there's probably no better way to overcome this fear than to actively seek accountability, whether from a peer-to-peer accountability partner or from a teacher or mentor who exemplifies the qualities and skills you want to develop.

Your accountability partner or mentor will be able to speak the truth to you and point out when you're making excuses, as well as when you're allowing your fear of being blamed or accepting responsibility to hold you back. Ideally, you'll discover someone who isn't afraid to call you out and who will guide you through the process of accepting ownership and responsibility for your life and actions, one baby step at a time. It won't seem natural at first, but you can get there, especially with the aid of someone you like and trust.

Getting Rid Of Excuses

Amanda realised she needed to change her practice of making excuses and refusing to accept responsibility when she saw it was negatively hurting her life and relationships. She engaged a business coach to help her with direction and accountability, and her coach gradually helped her realise some of the ways she had been avoiding responsibility or making excuses in her life and consulting firm.

Amanda found it difficult to accept that criticism and take more responsibility for her actions, but as she practised having a no-excuses mindset, first for little decisions and then for larger ones, she began to experience a new feeling of freedom and strength.

Her first truly significant breakthrough occurred when she was working with a consultancy client. She had just given many options for the firm when the CEO went to her and said, "What do you think we should do?"

Amanda would normally have avoided addressing the question by stating the alternatives and stressing that she was simply there to consult. Amanda, on the other hand, looked the CEO in the eyes and stated, "If it were my firm, I would certainly choose option A, and that's what I think you should do."

The CEO agreed, thanked her for her advice, and then added, "And here I was thinking you were going to be one of those consultants who never truly provides their opinion."

Amanda realised over time that her clients preferred honest opinions, even if they were occasionally incorrect, over wishy-washy counsel that didn't help them make a decision. She learned that they valued her readiness to speak out and that they seldom held it against her when she made a mistake as long as she was prepared to accept responsibility for it.

Taking control got simpler and easier as time passed.

Amanda's husband began to notice the difference at home as well, and he nearly fell out of his chair the day Amanda remarked, "You know what, you're right! I should not have done it, and I apologise. It was entirely my fault."

Amanda now maintains a sign over her desk that says "No Excuses" as a constant reminder to take full responsibility for the decisions she makes. She realises how trapped she had been by her fear of being blamed, and she vows never to return.

9

Fear Of Adversity

BRENDA HAS a profound feeling that the deck has always been set against her. And, while she wouldn't confess it to anybody, she frequently feels like she's simply fighting to stay alive without getting pushed down again.

Her family life was extremely chaotic while growing up, and she remembers yearning and begging for her family to be normal. Brenda's friends all seemed to have ideal parents and lifestyles, but her father drank too much, and her mother was constantly utterly stressed. While her parents were not impoverished, she saw that they were constantly concerned about money and battled. Brenda's parents separated while she was in sixth grade. Brenda was so embarrassed that she never informed anybody and avoided bringing friends around so that no one would find out about her secret.

She attended University and was doing well until her second year when she had Glandular Fever. She had practically little energy for months and could hardly make it to class. Her grades began to deteriorate, and she eventually lost her scholarship. The University was too expensive for her to continue without the scholarship, so she had to drop out. She started to work full-time as a receptionist at an office after graduating from high school. She believed she'd be able to work her way up the corporate ladder, but after being turned up for two promotions because her boss didn't like her, she decided to seek other opportunities. She enrolled in night sessions at a local cosmetology school and studied to become an aesthetician before landing a position at a nearby hotel spa.

She realised that she enjoyed and was skilled at assisting others with their skin problems. She built a devoted clientele, even though she felt more like a therapist than an aesthetician at times—people were continually revealing their marital woes! Brenda was a wonderful listener most of the time, which is why people opened up to her.

Brenda and a handful of coworkers decided to go out on their own and start a small massage and skincare clinic after working at the spa for a few years. Things were going well during the first few years, but Brenda saw that her two business partners were getting closer, and it felt like they were closing her out. She saw them meeting without her and making business choices without discussing her a couple of times, and things started to grow heated.

Brenda then took a month-long vacation in Europe, which she had been preparing for years. Her partners were meant to cover her clients while she was away, but instead, they took over the entire company and kicked Brenda out.

Brenda was heartbroken.

She sobbed for three days, unable to comprehend how anybody could be so cruel and self-centred. She eventually returned to work at the hotel spa, but the bitterness and resentment made it difficult for her to enjoy her profession. While her customers discuss their issues, she can't help but roll her eyes when they aren't looking. If only they realised what the true issues were!

Brenda feels that she's tried everything to go ahead, but she's just getting pushed back down. What's the purpose of even attempting when life is so unjust? She's had enough of putting herself out there and being heartbroken as a result. There doesn't appear to be a suitable answer, and she is frightened of putting in the effort just to be misled or shot down. She is afraid of hardship since her life has been nothing but difficult.

Brenda is a Pessimist.

The Pessimist Prototype

The Pessimist prototype, who is frequently a victim of events beyond her control, struggles most with the fear of adversity, typically showing itself as the fear of suffering through difficult times or the fear of pain. Because the Pessimist has had some difficulty, tragedy, or struggle in her life, whether lately or in the past, she has genuine grounds to feel victimised. But allowing oneself to remain in the victim position is precisely what keeps the Pessimist trapped.

Pessimists are easily derailed by any tough or challenging situations that come their way because they are so scared of adversity and suffering and believe they do not influence their position. Pessimists regard their misfortunes and struggles as acceptable reasons to quit or not attempt at all rather than as opportunities for growth and persistence.

Pessimists are frequently unable or unwilling to confront their situation front-on, preferring to withdraw to prevent more misery. Surprisingly, this response frequently worsens the situation. Perspective or seeing beyond one's own suffering, misery, and tough circumstances might be difficult for the Pessimist. Everyone else may have it easier than she does or that she has gotten the short end of the stick. It's also possible that she can't perceive herself as a victim.

The Pessimist might appear bitter at times, and she frequently believes she has been dealt a worse hand than others, leading her to believe that life is inherently unjust. The Pessimist likewise believes she is a victim of her circumstances and has little control over her future.

Not unexpectedly, the Pessimist fear prototype is one of the most difficult, if not the hardest, prototypes to own and embrace. Indeed, the most typical emotions to learning that one is a Pessimist are anger, denial, and resentment. Nobody likes to perceive themselves as pessimists or victims, especially if that is what keeps them trapped. It's important to note that the Pessimist fear prototype isn't any better or worse than the other fear prototypes. They all hold us back somehow, and we all have a little piece of every prototype inside of us.

The Pessimist is the least frequent fear prototype, with 3.4 per cent identifying it as their top prototype and 16.9 per cent identifying it as one of their top three.

Positive Characteristics

Pessimists are often sympathetic and generous. They are frequently told to put their heart on their sleeve and feel things more profoundly and strongly than others. As a result, they are typically extremely loving, sympathetic, and kind, with a great deal of empathy for others. They are usually quite friendly, good listeners, and maybe thoughtful and contemplative.

Pessimists are typically drawn to jobs that need them to care for and engage with others and those that involve contemplation and creative expression. Nursing, caregiving, social work, physical therapy, counselling, cosmetology, massage therapy, aesthetics, art, teaching, and writing are all common professional choices.

Behaviours And Habits

- Has a hard time moving on from unpleasant experiences in the past.
- She frequently believes that there are no solutions to her difficulties.
- Sees adversity as a roadblock rather than a stepping stone.
- Thinks she has it worse than most individuals she knows.
- Frequently believes that events outside her control stop her from attaining her goals.
- Can shut down in the face of hardship or difficulties.
- Is more prone to give up than persevere when things become tough.
- Tends to experience emotions more deeply than others.
- Is susceptible to criticism and adversity.
- She might get caught up in her own thoughts at times.
- Avoids taking risks regularly.

The Voice Of The Pessimist

Here are some of the opinions and views revealed by survey respondents who scored high on the Pessimist scale:

- "I'm concerned that what I want to achieve will be too difficult."
- "I don't want to waste all that time and effort just to get shot down again."
- "My first pregnancy was tough. My doctor did not listen to me, and I was unhappy while under his care, but no one did. My kid died during birth because I did not switch providers. I wish I had spoken out and trusted my instincts. Since then, I've been heartbroken by her death."
- "The thing that holds me back is my life—I've had cancer, I've had to care for my elderly parents, and my family has never had money. There are certain things I would want to accomplish, but they are just not possible."
- "I'm sick of trying and failing. I simply don't want to do it any longer."
- "I'm frightened of adding more work and time when I'm always exhausted, not knowing if it'll be worth it in the end. It's stressful to be the primary breadwinner as well as the wife and mother. With a special needs child who cannot be left alone—even as a teenager—I rarely have time to do anything pleasant for myself. Not to mention my ageing parents and the state of my house."
- "After a vehicle accident terminated my dancing career and the economy fell at the same time, I was left with a mountain of problems. Due to my injuries, I was unable to operate the firm. Due to injuries, I was unable to dance. I was trapped, unsure of where to go or how to go on in my life. It trapped me in time for years and continues to hold me back in many ways."
- "I don't want to give my husband any more fuel. He doesn't believe in me; therefore, I don't think I can accomplish it."
- "I am always trying new things, but old difficulties continually come in the way and weigh me down."

How This Fear Can Hold You Back

Perception is reality and the sense that life isn't fair or that you've had it harder than others may be crushing for the Pessimist prototype. This emotion or perception frequently results from truly tough circumstances—tragedy, sickness, betrayal, or loss—that you are fighting to overcome.

It's critical to understand that your feelings of grief, rage, and hatred are valid and sometimes even justified. Allowing oneself to be trapped due to challenging circumstances, on the other hand, is not serving you and may be holding you back. Here are some of the ways that being a pessimist may harm you and keep you stuck:

- You are often disheartened and have difficulty overcoming obstacles and hardship. Instead, you find yourself trapped or annoyed in the "messy middle."
- You may occasionally get into a cycle of self-pity and a "poor me" mindset, feeling that life is unjust or that your circumstances are worse than those of others. While this may or may not be true, feeling sorry for yourself simply serves to keep you back.
- When you believe you have been wronged, you may struggle with forgiving and showing others grace.
- You may find it difficult to establish positive connections with those who you believe have it better than you. Because you have a propensity to regard life as unfair, you may be envious of others who appear to have been dealt a better hand.
- Your aversion to pain and hardship may drive you to avoid taking chances, even minor ones, or pursuing large goals and aspirations since even the notion of effort is unpleasant.
- When you anticipate that something will be difficult, you may experience worry and fear.
- You may let preconceived notions about what has occurred to you, your life circumstances, or how people

have treated you in the past determine what you feel you are capable of.

Methods For Overcoming This Fear

Here are a few ideas for overcoming your fear of adversity.

Reframe

Adversity is never enjoyable. Illness, tragedy, abuse, betrayal, despair, financial trouble, disappointments, errors, blunders, and hardships—the list of heinous things that may and do happen in life is nearly infinite. The majority of them are things we wouldn't want on our worst enemy. You've probably already been through a lot of misfortune, which has made you fearful of going through more. Even Nevertheless, there is nearly always something positive that may arise from tragedy or adversity. Instead of viewing difficulties as roadblocks, you may learn to see them as stepping stones to where you need to go.

No, making errors or going through tragedy and sorrow is not enjoyable. However, it is critical not to let the fear of overcoming hardship prevent you from going for it or attempting new things.

A large portion of your fear stems from the script that has been playing within your brain, which implies that if you want to break this fear, you must begin playing a new message. If you have a deep-seated belief that you have been dealt a bad hand, what can you say yourself to assist you in the beginning to change your mind? Similarly, if you're experiencing anger or bitterness as a result of how you've been treated, or if you've suffered from the sensation that life isn't fair, it's time to start rewriting the message you're playing inside your brain.

Positive affirmations that you repeat to yourself might sometimes suffice. Other times, finding more positive messages to listen to, such as those found on audiobooks or podcasts, may be necessary. It might imply seeking spiritual guidance through Scripture, worship, or a spiritual counsellor. It may even necessitate the services of a therapist or counsellor.

TAKE INITIATIVE

Feeling as if you've had to deal with a slew of unjust or harsh situations that are entirely beyond your control is a significant signal of the Pessimist pattern. And, while you may not always be able to change your circumstances—what happens to you or how others treat you—you can always control how you respond.

The Pessimist, like the Excuse Maker, must create an internal centre of control. While it may appear frightening at first, recognising that you can declare that no matter who mistreated you or what awful things occurred to you, you still have a choice is freeing! When you regain control of your response, you no longer have to be concerned about what happens to you, how other people treat you, or what difficulties may arise since it is still your life and no one else's.

ESTABLISH ACCOUNTABILITY

When faced with tragedy, disease, or other misfortune, it can be difficult to gain perspective, to "see the forest for the trees." At the moment, it feels like the deck has been loaded against you—life isn't fair, and things are much worse for you than they are for others. But the fact is that, while everyone's suffering and adversity appear a bit different, everyone experiences difficulty and adversity. Even though their conflicts take place behind closed doors, no one is immune. Take comfort in the fact that you are not alone, and actively seek out friends or accountability partners who can assist you in gaining that outside perspective.

Depending on your situation, you may want to explore joining a support group—you can find groups for everything from grief and substance addiction to depression and debt relief, among other things. A support group can help you remember that others have been down this road before you, and it may even suggest ideas you hadn't considered.

Getting Over Pessimism

Brenda decided to seek outside assistance after recognising she was plunging deeper and deeper into a hole of bitterness and resentment. She began visiting a counsellor, who assisted her in gaining a better understanding of the chaotic childhood she had always perceived. Brenda started to see that her parents, while far from ideal, had done their best and had done many things correctly. She began to feel more compassion for the tension they must have both felt and even had a heart-to-heart with her mother, which provided a lot of light on situations she hadn't comprehended as a child.

She also worked through her resentment of being forced to drop out of University, and she was surprised to eventually confess to herself that she hadn't enjoyed it and that the true reason her grades began to slide was that she wasn't interested in the subjects she had been taking. She also discovered how much she enjoyed aesthetics and couldn't imagine doing anything else for a living. It felt like a weight had been lifted for Brenda since when she reflected on her University experience, she was happy that her brush with Glandular Fever had helped her discover an alternative route.

Brenda still felt a lot of resentment against her business partners, but her counsellor helped her understand that resentment was eating her up inside and wasn't serving her well. She made the intentional decision to forgive them and move on. It wasn't easy, and it took Brenda a long time and a lot of prayers, but the anger gradually subsided.

Brenda, on the other hand, immersed herself in servicing her guests at the hotel spa. She rose to the position of top aesthetician on the team, quadruple her rates, and was the first to have her waiting list. The hotel management even named her Employee of the Year.

Brenda now realises how much her fear of hardship was holding her back, and she is resolved to never again let events she cannot control dictate the things she can.

10

Continue To Be Optimistic

LET US NOT DELUDE OURSELVES. It's not for the faint of heart to do it frightened. It is not always simple to face our fears and pursue our great ambitions and desires. In reality, that is rarely the case.

After all, if it were simple, everyone would do it. It wouldn't be remarkable, significant, or notable if it were simple. It wouldn't be worth fighting for if it were simple. And, while most of us certainly realise that doing it afraid is difficult, it's not always simple to remember in practice. When things get difficult or when disappointments and hurdles appear, the optimism and excitement we had at the start are quickly replaced by discouragement, frustration, and fear.

We don't want it to be difficult. We don't want it to be painful. We don't want to get our hands filthy, the battle for what we want, or experience the crushing disappointment or shame of failure. We don't want to confront challenges or be evaluated by others. We don't want to have to accept responsibility or discover that we may not be capable of achieving our goals.

When things get rough, it cannot be easy to stay positive. But this is precisely the time when you want encouragement the most. And, while you might sit about hoping and praying for that encouragement to come from someplace or someone else, the fact is that you will most likely be waiting a very long time.

Remember that the only thing you can ever control is yourself—not what happens to you, but how you respond to it. That means one of the most important things you can do for yourself is learn how to set protections in place to help you avoid and overcome discouragement while also finding greater joy along the road.

Beware Of The Space Between

When it comes to living a life we enjoy, identifying and committing to significant goals is essential. They are the catalysts that spark a fire in our bellies, tighten our chests, and push us to achieve and be more than we ever imagined we were capable of. They provide us with something to aim at and a purpose to get out of bed in the morning.

But, as essential as they are, such noble goals also represent a risk.

Have you ever observed that there appears to be a shiny wet patch ahead when driving on a hot, sunny day? A highway mirage occurs when "convection causes the temperature of the air to change, and the difference between the hot air near the surface of the road and the denser cool air above it generates a gradient in the refractive index of the air," according to Wikipedia.

The most irritating aspect of this illusion is that you can never get to it. It's always someplace up ahead, far off on the horizon, no matter how long or far you drive. Unfortunately, our lofty ambitions might sometimes feel like a highway mirage, always just out of grasp. Because they appear so far away, they become a source of irritation and despair rather than motivation. When that tumultuous middle stage arrives, and things begin to get difficult, unpleasant, and intense, it's natural to become disheartened or certain you'll never get there.

It's all too easy to get stuck in "the space between," that area between where you are and where you want to go. It's that spot where you have all these lofty aspirations, and there's always more to do to get there, but you never quite get there. We will never feel like we are moving anywhere or doing anything if we spend all our time in this area. That is why it is critical to take time each day to look back rather than solely forward, celebrate your victories and successes rather than always focus on all the things you haven't done yet.

Having clear objectives is fantastic, and being goal-oriented can be a tremendous strength, but failing to focus on what you've already done and what you're continuing to accomplish—even if you're not quite there yet—may easily drag you down.

Finally, it would help if you found delight in the trip, not simply the goal. And the only way to do it is to avoid the area in between. Yes, take a risk and look forward to discovering what's possible. But don't forget to look back and evaluate how far you've come.

Modify The Script

That voice is present in all of us. It might be telling us that we don't deserve to ask for a raise or that we aren't as talented, funny, or well-spoken as a coworker. It may be saying things like, "You're not a good mom," "You're a lousy cleaner," "You'll never be organised," or "You completely suck at maths." It might be telling us that we can't get out of debt or that we're not clever enough to succeed. It might mean that we are too busy to pursue our major goals and dreams or that we don't have time to read, learn, or do anything for ourselves.

That voice might be cautioning us not to do new things or take risks because we could fail. Or the caution might be that we are afraid to reach out and seek help for fear of being rejected. It might advise us not to devote all of our attention and effort to achieving our dreams since we don't know what others think. "What if they don't understand?" it sighs, "or what if they mock me?"

Whatever your inner voice tells you, and whatever your limiting beliefs are, I promise they are present. And, while we can't always avoid those limiting ideas or the voice in our ear from appearing, we can refuse to listen to them! Our limiting ideas have so much power over us because we don't know that what we hear in our brains isn't always based on reality but rather on fear.

We just think that the message we are hearing—the voice, the thought, the limiting belief—is our reality, while in fact, it is nothing more than that: a voice, an idea, or a limiting belief. Just because a voice in our heads tells us something is true, it does not imply it is. In reality, it's not always true—almost usually, I'd say.

It's only an idea. But when we name the fear driving the limiting belief or the voice in our brain, once we see a limiting belief for what it is—just a thought that is holding us back—we can deprive it of its power and move past it. That's when we may say, "That voice in my brain tells me I'm not clever enough to succeed, but it's actually because I'm afraid of making a mistake." But even the brightest individuals make mistakes, and it is through their failures that they learn."

It's known as changing the script. You know, the self-talk message that's been playing over and over in your brain. The one who tells you that you're not good enough, clever enough, or attractive enough, or that you'll never succeed, or that you'll never get organised, or that you can't write, or that you shouldn't even try.

The script keeps telling you that you can't. If you wish to cease listening to that message, you must find a means to replace it with a new one.

Consider this. If your present self-talk is training your brain to think untrue facts about yourself, the easiest approach to reprogram your brain is to begin replacing the negative self-talk messages with something fresh. Something that is, in fact, true. We need to start changing the message that is being broadcast into something that isn't so self-defeating. Change the script, and you will, without a doubt, change your viewpoint.

Continue Filling Up

As humans, we have an unquenchable desire for encouragement. It doesn't seem to matter how many times we are told that we are clever, capable, attractive, courageous, or any other number of good messages; we still need to hear it over and over. We forget it as soon as we hear it again. When life becomes chaotic, difficult, or stressful, self-doubt and all of those fears seep in. And then our confidence begins to dwindle once more.

That is why it is critical to keep filling up. There is no limit to how many motivational and self-help books you should read, how many times you should read your favourite Bible verses or devotionals, how many inspirational podcasts you should listen to, or how many events or gatherings you should attend because the energy and excitement, motivation and inspiration that feel so incredible at the moment will fade. Even still, the more positive and encouraging messages you receive, the more likely you are to keep some of them.

It would help if you continued to fill up. Make it a habit to listen to podcasts when driving, exercising, or washing the chores. (The Do It Scared podcast is a good place to start!) Make it a goal to read at least one uplifting book every month, or just reread your favourites. Look for activities and gatherings in your region that will energise you and allow you to meet like-minded individuals. Make time to spend with friends and mentors who you know will both challenge and support you.

Make keeping motivated a priority, as well as encouraging and inspiring others so that the progress you've made doesn't go away.

Practice Self-Care

The idea is not so much what you do to take care of yourself as you make time for yourself without feeling bad about it.

Because the fact is that taking care of yourself is better for everyone. There is the immediate benefit of having fun and doing anything you want at the time. You're overjoyed. You take a deep breath and smile. However, the stress of ignoring your own needs has long-term detrimental repercussions on your health, mind, and spirit. When we are overburdened, we are unable to offer our all to anybody or anything. Allowing ourselves a little "me time" now and then acts as a release valve for all the stress that accumulates. It gives us more energy and less fatigue, boosts our immune system, and makes us feel calmer, gentler, and more in control of our emotions.

Taking time to care for our own well-being also restores our ability to care for the people in our lives—our spouse, children, friends, and extended family. Because those closest to us endure the brunt of our stress, they stand to profit the most from our self-care.

While it may appear selfish or indulgent at the moment, it is not. Remember the oxygen mask principle on an aeroplane? When you fix your own mask before aiding others, you are performing one of the least selfish acts you can perform.

Every Victory Should Be Celebrated

Bravery is a daily decision that necessitates the courage to act, even in the face of fear, and to continue taking steps toward your goals, even when you're not always sure where the route will go. Even while you work toward your objectives, it's easy to lose sight of how far you've come, which is why it's critical to remember to look both forward and back. So keep track of your accomplishments. Maintain a thankfulness diary or a success log, and remember to appreciate your victories along the road. Create fresh self-talk scripts that are truthful and honest to encourage you. Take proper care of yourself. And don't lose hope.

Finally, keep in mind that this book is not meant to be a passive read but rather one that inspires you to take action in your own life. If you haven't already, I strongly advise you to use the materials in this book.

Because you are stronger than you believe, you can do it, and you can do it while afraid. And if you keep going no matter what, you'll move one step closer to living the life you want.

Feedback

Thank you for reading 'Start Being Fearless, Stop Being Scared'. We hope you enjoyed the book? Please now scan the QR code below to leave your feedback.

Claim Your Freebie NOW!

Get Good At Problem Solving

Want to know the secret behind getting good at problem solving? Everyone seems to be able to do it, but you're stuck in the pile of endless to-do lists with little progress.

Ok, so how do I get my FREE book?

EASY! See the next page

Claim Your Freebie NOW

Instructions:

1. Open the camera or the QR reader application on your smartphone.
2. Point your camera at the QR code to scan the QR code.
3. A notification will pop-up on screen.
4. Click on the notification to open the website link

Also By Rachel Stone

How To Remove Negativity From Your Life

Rid yourself forever from the negative thoughts that plague your life with this amazing, life-changing book.

Also By Rachel Stone

Why Living a Simple Life is Better for You

An easy guide to help you change the way you think about your life. Take steps to start living a stress-free life.

Also By Rachel Stone

How To Heal Toxic Thoughts

Are you sick of your whole day being ruined due to your overthinking? Have you had enough of self-sabotaging everything good in your life? Do you want practical strategies to finally have a peaceful night's sleep?

Grab the Rachel Stone series NOW

Instructions:

1. Open the camera or the QR reader application on your smartphone.
2. Point your camera at the QR code to scan the QR code.
3. A notification will pop-up on screen.
4. Click on the notification to open the website link

www.ingramcontent.com/pod-product-compliance
Lightning Source LLC
Chambersburg PA
CBHW031546080526
44588CB00018B/2712